STRENGTHENING YOUR

Marriage

AND FAMILY

STRENGTHENING YOUR

Marriage

AND FAMILY

DOUGLAS E. BRINLEY

Bookcraft
Salt Lake City, Utah

Library of Congress Catalog Card Number: 94-71583

ISBN 1-57008-308-8

Third Printing, 1999

Printed in the United States of America

Contents

Acknowledgments

Someone has said that writing a book is similar to a pregnancy—you feel all the sensations and kicking as you go along, and you are anxious to see what the final product looks like. Both are somewhat magical processes, it seems, that come together after sufficient "labor pains." There is some discomfort in both, but when it is all over, you feel that it wasn't that bad and before long you are thinking that you might do it again sometime!

My thanks to Cory Maxwell of Bookcraft for his encouragement and interest in this effort, and to Garry Garff and Rebecca Taylor for their editing skills. Dan Hogan helped in some early editing, as did my wife, Geri. I extend appreciation to Brigham Young University for funds to assist me in research and supplies.

My genuine thanks also go to the Prophet Joseph Smith, who restored the concept of eternal marriage and eternal lives in this final dispensation, and to subsequent prophets, who have clarified the place of marriage and family in this mortal adventure. As Latter-day Saints, we have the opportunity to show the world that we can marry, have a number of offspring, and still smile, that marital happiness is the epitome of joy, and that righteous children are the source of our rejoicing. Anything else will slow the establishment of Zion.

Introduction

Paul and Clara were an older couple who had been married for over thirty-five years. As I visited with them on several occasions, it became clear to me that their marriage was a disaster and had been for many years. Yet they had stayed together and reared a number of children. Though they were religiously active, their marriage, from nearly every aspect, was in shambles. As I met with them several times, they seemed intent on cataloging each other's sins in front of me. As soon as one took a breath, the other began his or her list of offenses.

I listened patiently until I felt that I had the courage to intervene, and interrupted their mutual bash session. "Excuse me," I said, "but in observing you two, I'd like to share an observation. You realize, of course, that in what I say I am not the final judge; the Lord will do that. But if the Judgment were held today, and the Lord called me to be a witness, let me tell you what I would say that I see. I would say that you both seem to have set a course for the telestial kingdom. I think the two of you have offended the Spirit of the Lord so badly by the way you treat each other that surely the heavens must weep at what they see. You have had the gospel your entire lives, yet you have missed its major theme. You have become so critical and devastating in your comments to each other that you ought to be

1

ashamed to call yourselves Latter-day Saints. And if I am embarrassed at the way you censure each other, I can imagine how the Lord must feel.

"Paul," I said, looking him straight in the eye, "I don't think you understand the nature of the priesthood you hold. You have made a mockery of its beauty, influence, and power, especially as it relates to being Clara's husband.

"Clara," I said, turning to her, "after all these years of living with Paul, you seem to have no idea what makes a man tick, how to lift and inspire him to be a better companion to you."

Looking at both of them now, I continued: "The two of you have used your marital years to destroy rather than strengthen each other. Consequently, as I see it, you have only another twenty, maybe thirty years left to live with each other. Then one of you will die and that will be the end of your experience with marriage. Never again, through all eternity, will either of you live in a marriage relationship. I think"—I paused, hoping this next thought would sink in—"you will look back at these years with sadness for what might have been. I think you two will wish that you had made some different choices along the way. Of course, you have your agency; you may do as you please. And up until now you seem to have wanted to use it to devastate each other.

"On the other hand," I said, in an effort to bring something positive out of the whole mess, "wouldn't it be great on Judgment Day to have the Lord say, 'You two had a rough thirty-five years, didn't you! And then you made some wonderful changes. You came to realize what mortal life, agency, and my atonement were all about, and the past thirty years have been a complete reversal from those earlier ones. Thank you for making the necessary changes! Thank you for doing what needed to be done in order to qualify for the highest degree of the celestial kingdom. Thank you for making my atonement worth the effort. I want to welcome you into a society of people who love their companions as you two now do, a society of couples who have conducted their lives so that they want and are eligible to be together forever.'"

I waited, holding my breath, thinking that they might run out the door offended. Instead, to my surprise, they both bowed their heads and began to weep. Paul took Clara's hand

and apologized—right there in front of me. She reached out to him and accepted his embrace. Both admitted that the Lord must be disappointed with them; that they had treated each other terribly; that they had a long way to go but that they could do better—indeed, they *would* do better. Their apologies were accepted, and forgiveness was extended. They committed to each other that they would make the necessary changes. They seemed determined to turn things around.

When we run into each other on occasion, they seem grateful to me for helping them make some needed changes, but all I did was to remind them of the goal of eternal life they could reach if they would change directions. I think they are going to make it. I honestly believe that the little bit of theology that I rehearsed to them that day shocked them into realizing that eternity is a long time to be alone, and that if they wanted to avoid such a fate they needed to use the opportunity of this earth life to prepare for a life together in eternity.

Now, I suppose that professional counselors would not make any money if they made a practice of talking like this to people; not many couples would likely sit there and take it as these two people did. But what I told Paul and Clara I believe to be true. If our hearts are not right, if our spirits are not softened, if our perspective is not grounded in an eternal framework, if we are not developing in more Christlike ways, if our behavior does not match our knowledge, there will be no *long-range* improvement in our family relationships, to say nothing of eternal opportunities. Oh yes, we can be nice and decent for short periods of time. We can control our behavior for a week or two, maybe even a couple of months. We can behave decently enough when we want sexual favors from our spouses or when we want to impress the neighbors or the boss. But if we are to become eligible for exaltation, it will take more than Band-Aids and quick apologies designed simply to "get someone off my back." We cannot slip past the Holy Ghost into the celestial kingdom. We must actually *be* celestial people.

Now, this doesn't mean that we must be perfect in this life, thank goodness. But the Savior worked out the Atonement for us that we might apply it in our lives to purge out of our natures those traits which prevent us from reaching a celestial standard. If we are not making use of the opportunities thus afforded us, if we are not making steady progress as companions and parents, then perhaps Satan is carefully leading us down to hell while we think we are on the strait and narrow path (see 2 Nephi 28:21).

A major point about all of this is that Paul and Clara didn't need to have communication therapy for years or counseling for months to turn their lives around. What they needed was renewed perspective, a softened heart, restored commitment. Their marriage was worth saving. They knew better than anyone else that they were deeply hurting each other, and that they could stop these senseless choices that produced the inevitable hurtful consequences—if they wanted to. Once they knew where they wanted to go and what it would take to get there, they were free agents and could do it. They possessed the necessary skills to succeed. They had been practicing adequate communication patterns for years *with everyone else but each other.* And I was left with the impression of how powerful the restored gospel really is when its light is focused on improving marriage and family relations.

I first became interested in how couples go from marriage to divorce years ago when two good friends, married only a few years, decided to split up. I could not imagine these two divorcing. I attended their wedding. On that day they were excited to begin life together on an eternal footing in the temple. But how quickly it seemed to turn! In only a few short years, here they were dividing up property and children as if these were so much chattel. I was reminded of something that President Joseph Fielding Smith had said that I had read years before while serving as a missionary. It had impressed me then and set the tone for my own commitment to be the best marriage partner I could be.

> If all mankind would live in strict obedience to the gospel, and in that love which is begotten by the Spirit of the Lord, all marriages would be eternal, divorce would be unknown. Divorce is not part of the gospel plan and has been introduced because of the hardness of heart and unbelief of the people.
>
> When the Pharisees tempted Christ saying: "Is it lawful for a man to put away his wife for every cause," he answered them: "Have ye not read, that he which made them at the beginning made them male and female, And said, For this cause shall a man leave father and mother, and shall cleave to his wife: and they

twain shall be one flesh? Wherefore they are no more twain, but one flesh. What therefore God hath joined together, let no man put asunder." . . .

There never could be a divorce in this Church if the husband and wife were keeping the commandments of God. . . .

. . . A man would not get tired of his wife, if he had the love of God in his heart. A woman would not get tired of her husband, if she had in her heart the love of God, that first of all commandments. They could not do it! . . .

. . . We have cases, perhaps, where a woman is justified in seeking relief, to be separated from a brutal husband who lives after the flesh, whose incontinency is such that he makes her life miserable; and they are not keeping the commandments that were given to them when they were married in the temple for time and all eternity, where he is supposed to love and respect and care for his wife with all the humility, in all the faith, and the understanding of the gospel of Jesus Christ. . . .

Now I realize that there are some cases where a wife needs to have a separation, perhaps a husband should have a separation, but always because of a violation, a serious violation of the covenants that have been made. . . .

If you want to know how serious it is to seek a divorce, I want you to read what the Lord says in the Sermon on the Mount, which is repeated in the Book of Mormon in a similar sermon that was given to the Nephites. If we understood, if we comprehended what the Lord says there, I want to tell you, people would be frightened rather than to seek a separation on some trivial matter—they would be frightened.

Marriage according to the law of the Church is the most holy and sacred ordinance. It will bring to the husband and the wife, if they abide in their covenants, the fulness of exaltation in the kingdom of God. When that covenant is broken, it will bring eternal misery to the guilty party, for we will all have to answer for our deeds done while in the flesh. It is an ordinance that cannot be trifled with, and the covenants made in the temple cannot be broken without dire punishment to the one who is guilty.

When a couple are married in the temple, they should try to live in peace and harmony, and if both are faithful members of the Church, this should not be impossible. Young people should try to tolerate each other's weaknesses and overcome them. If they live worthy of exaltation, they will enter the celestial kingdom without the frailties and weaknesses of mortality and will be perfect. (*Doctrines of Salvation*, comp. Bruce R. McConkie, 3 vols. [Salt Lake City: Bookcraft, 1954–56], 2:80–81, 82, 83–84.)

This perspective has become my theme song—as you will see. I am convinced that the major cause of our marriage and family troubles as Latter-day Saints is that we separate doctrine from practice. Though we discuss doctrine in our Church meetings—most active Latter-day Saints could pass a paper-pencil test on the basics—we often fail to see how to implement these principles in our families. We do apply them with other people, however. In many instances we treat everyone else better than we do the members of our own families. Have you noticed how well we behave at ward functions, in social situations, and public places? There we are generally gracious and kind and even Christlike. But as I listen to people describe marital problems, it is apparent that they do not practice at the hearth the same principles they do in the public domain.

My hope in preparing this book has been that it might, through the principles and examples presented, prove helpful to those seeking to become better companions and parents. After all, we are involved in a great adventure: to seek a compatible spouse, to marry and share in the exquisite joys of our male and female natures, and to conceive, bear, and rear faithful children who will repeat the same cycle through which we all pass. Most needed are a gospel perspective and a humble heart that desires strongly to succeed.

Don't be impatient with the theology I review here, for it will be your friend and assist you in your fantastic journey. Perhaps a new thought will burrow its way into your soul and become a catalyst for you to be a more committed partner on the path to eternal life.

Using a separate sheet of paper, respond to the following questions alone. Add whatever comments you think would be helpful to explain your selection or feelings. If you feel comfortable, share your answers with your spouse and together discuss ways to improve your relationship.

How Satisfying to Me Is My Marriage?

1. *We have been married:*

Less than a year	_____	11–19 years	_____
1–5 years	_____	Over 20 years	_____
6–10 years	_____	Over 30 years	_____

2. *I would describe my marriage and my feelings about it this way:*

_____

_____

_____

3. *I think my spouse would describe our marriage this way:*

_____

_____

_____

4. *How easy is it to risk my personal thoughts and feelings with him/her?*

Very easy _____   Somewhat difficult _____
Fairly easy _____   Very difficult   _____
*Comments:*_____

_____

5. *What topics seem difficult for us to discuss together, and why?*

Emotional   Unhappiness at
   problems _____   home/work   _____
Children   _____   Money concerns   _____
Sexual topics   _____   Religious concerns _____
Hopes and dreams _____   Investments   _____
Other: _____
Why so difficult to discuss? _____

_____

_____

_____

6. *The words that best describe my relationship with my spouse are:*

Warm and   Conflict-ridden,
   companionable _____   tense   _____
Passionate   _____   Convenient   _____
Fun   _____   Unexciting, boring _____
Other: _____
*Comments:*_____

_____

_____

7. *In order to improve my marriage I need to:*

_____

_____

_____
_____
_____
_____
_____

8. *In what ways, if any, has my marriage not lived up to my expectations?*
   My partner takes me for granted   _____
   We have grown apart emotionally   _____
   We don't have the same goals   _____
   We seldom talk about things that matter   _____
   We don't spend much time together   _____
   He/she is more interested in work/home than me   _____
   I feel alone in my marriage   _____
   We never get off alone together   _____
   I act just like my parents   _____
   He/she acts just like his/her parents   _____
   I am not giving our marriage my best efforts   _____
   Other: _____
   Comments:_____
   _____
   _____

9. *My marriage can be described in the following terms:*
   A business arrangement, exchange of services   _____
   The fire has gone out   _____
   We have a blazing romance   _____
   We had it at one time, but we have lost it   _____
   We struggled at first, but now we are together   _____
   We love each other and talk about everything   _____
   Other: _____
   Comments:_____
   _____
   _____

10. *I have personally gained or enjoyed in marriage:*
    Greater emotional security and stability   _____
    A closeness, an understanding "best friend"   _____
    Self-confidence   _____
    Broader interests, friendships   _____

Financial security   _____
A sense of purpose   _____
Sexual fulfillment   _____
Other: _____
*Comments:*_____
_____
_____

11. *I am most happy with my marriage/spouse when:*
_____
_____
_____

12. *I am most frustrated or discouraged with my marriage/spouse when:*_____
_____
_____
_____
_____
_____

13. *I would describe my feelings about our marital intimacy as:*
Very satisfying   ____   Somewhat dissatisfying ____
Reasonably satisfying ____   Quite dissatisfying   ____
Because: (check if your answer above was "Somewhat dissatisfying" or "Quite dissatisfying")
We are too hurried   _____
The experience is too mechanical   _____
My spouse is not responsive to my needs   _____
My spouse is not spontaneous   _____
There is too frequent sexual activity   _____
My spouse is too demanding about sex   _____
There is too infrequent sexual activity   _____
I never reach a climax/orgasm   _____
Age and physical problems make it hard   _____
Over the years I have lost interest   _____
Write a paragraph or two about intimacy in your marriage (include such matters as frequency, satisfaction, suggestions for spouse, suggestions of how you might enjoy each other more, fears, worries):
_____
_____
_____

_____
_____
_____
_____

14. *How committed am I to my marriage?*
    I think I am more committed to our
        marriage than my spouse   _____
    My spouse is more committed to our
        marriage than I am   _____
    I don't see how we can make it   _____
    We make a great couple   _____
    I don't think my spouse wants to be married to me _____
    I love my spouse and am thankful that we are sealed _____
    I like my spouse most of the time, but there are
        a number of things that need improvement, such as:

    _____
    _____

    Comments:_____
    _____
    _____

15. *What is my greatest fear/challenge with regard to my marital happiness?*
    His/her parents   _____   Lack of mutual trust _____
    Money   _____   Unsatisfactory sex   _____
    Health (spouse/mine) _____   Lack of excitement   _____
    Children/stepchildren _____   Mutual competition   _____
    Job/homemaking   _____   Church activity   _____
    Other: _____
    Comments:_____
    _____
    _____

16. *What are my spouse's greatest strengths?* (Multiple)
    Kindness and consideration   _____
    Sense of humor   _____
    Intelligence   _____
    Strongly masculine/feminine   _____
    Supportiveness   _____
    Sense of responsibility   _____

Integrity _____
Testimony _____
Tells me I'm attractive _____
Leads out in our family _____
Christlike _____
Capable father/mother _____
Sensitive to my needs _____
Ambitious _____
Other or Comments: _____

_____

_____

17. *My greatest strengths as a marriage partner are:* (Multiple)
   a. _____
   b. _____
   c. _____
   d. _____
   e. _____
18. *If I had a suggestion or two for my spouse, it would be:*
   Express feelings and emotions _____
   Control temper _____
   Help with household chores _____
   Be more involved (family) _____
   Talk about job and home life more _____
   Try new things (travel, hobby) _____
   Be interested in my interests _____
   Control excesses (eating, etc.) _____
   Increase nonsexual affection _____
   Spend time with children _____
   Spend more time with me _____
   Increase love, affection _____
   Be more socially outgoing _____
   Watch TV less _____
   Budget more wisely _____
   Treat my folks better _____
   Listen to my concerns _____
   Be more flexible _____
   Be less physical _____
   Be more punctual _____

Explain above, or list other suggestions I would give my spouse:

_____

_____

_____

_____

19. *Overall, I would rate my marriage as:* (Circle the number, 10 being the best)

    1   2   3   4   5   6   7   8   9   10

    Reasons for above number:

    _____

    _____

20. *What are our strengths and weaknesses as parents?*

    My strengths: _____

    _____

    _____

    *His/her strengths:*_____

    _____

    _____

    *My weaknesses:*_____

    _____

    _____

    His/her weaknesses: _____

    _____

    _____

CHAPTER ONE

The Importance of Family Relations

In the dispensation of the fulness of times, our goal as Latter-day Saints is to establish Zion, a people who will live the gospel in its fulness and prepare the way for the second coming of Jesus Christ. Our success in this effort is directly related to how well our homes reflect the ideals and standards of Zion, for "Zion cannot be built up unless it is by the principles of the law of the celestial kingdom" (D&C 105:5). Either our homes will be the seedbeds from which spring the pure in heart, or, in this day of wickedness, they will be the fields that bring forth not only tares but also briars, thistles, and noxious weeds. Husbands and wives are the caretakers of a little section of the Lord's vineyard, and the work of God in the last and final dispensation is, in large measure, in their hands.

Family life becomes the great adventure of mortality, for it is the first time in our individual existence that we have ever been allowed the privilege to marry and become parents. This is a new experience for all of us. Uniting two people in marriage is a profound undertaking that brings different sexes and unique backgrounds together in a union to challenge and yet enrich the lives of those two people beyond either one's wildest imaginings.

Through the experiences of marriage and parenthood, they will gain insights about themselves that will stretch their souls—all the way to exaltation. They are bound together by principle, ordinance, and covenant with God to form a unit of the celestial kingdom. Their children reflect both physical and spiritual images of their parents, as these youngsters too must pass through the divine curriculum.

Our dispensation mandate, the mission of the Church—to "invite all to come unto Christ" (D&C 20:59) "and be perfected in him" (Moroni 10:32)—with its three aspects of proclaiming the gospel to all the world (missionary work), perfecting the Saints (building Zion), and redeeming the dead, cannot be left to slackers. Those who would prefer to imbibe the ease and prosperity of our day will be easily distracted from the divine mission. For us to reach the lofty heights to which this dispensation has been ordained, the finest efforts of parents and children are now required. We are about our Father's business. Strong marriage partners and exemplary parents are wanted—in fact, demanded—for they hold the key to our success. Now and in the coming days and years, family members must be physically and mentally tough, spiritually sound, well trained and well versed in the mission and doctrines of the Church if they are to push forward the work of God. It is for each married couple to demonstrate that righteousness can be developed first in their family, then the neighborhood, the community, the nation, and, ultimately, the world.

That's the good news—that God has called us to labor in his vineyard. We are his representatives. The bad news, however, is that there are still too many parallels between us and those members in the early days of the restored Church of whom the Lord said, as they were forced to flee the promised land, "They have not learned to be obedient to the things which I required at their hands" (D&C 105:3). We must ask ourselves, Are we, as individuals, more obedient and faithful to the commands and counsel of living prophets than we were in our first attempt to build Zion, or could our goal be even more insurmountable today with our increased abundance, leisure time, political freedom, and shopping malls to distract us?

The Family "Garden"

The struggle is always with the laborers and their commitment to the harvest. They must have a vision of what their efforts will produce. They must want to be productive. Nurturing each tender seedling will require great effort on their part and will be essential if the yield is to be bounteous. Surely the seed is good, for a prophet, Ezra Taft Benson, declared, "Our young generation, as a group, is even more faithful than the older generation. God has reserved you for the eleventh hour—the great and dreadful day of the Lord. It will be your responsibility . . . to help bear off the kingdom of God triumphantly." (*The Teachings of Ezra Taft Benson* [Salt Lake City: Bookcraft, 1988], p. 558.)

Parents are the gardeners. They must prune and dig and prepare the soil. In our day, however, a number of adults have been unwilling to invest in seed and equipment (that is, they prefer to remain single), while some question the need to even plant a garden (they live together without marriage). Substantial numbers don't want to be bothered with any fruit this year or perhaps any year (indiscriminate birth control), and a growing force choose to destroy (through abortion) signs of new life and growth. For others, weeds are choking out the young sprouts, or insects (pornography and inappropriate music, videos, movies, and drugs) devour them before they reach full bloom.

Consequently, we must check the harvest for its quality, for Zion remains incomplete. Our past inability to establish Zion in Missouri could repeat itself if we are not careful. But that must not be. For if we are to be prepared for the monumental task we have committed ourselves to perform, the children of the rising generation will need two committed parents—ideally the same two who created them—who will explain to their understanding their latter-day destiny, their sacred mission. Who else, besides two committed parents with spiritual vision, could possibly have the interest and commitment to carry out this profound undertaking?

To raise up good seed, we need to check the farmer's almanac (scriptures) and consult experienced farmers (living prophets) who can foresee the major threats the growing season could bring. We cannot be satisfied with comparing this year's yield to last, or assume that "all is well" and that neighbors will secure the harvest if we are sidetracked. Any loss or damage to a prospective unit of the celestial kingdom threatens present and future yields. We are commissioned to develop the vineyard so that other gardeners—some inexperienced and others disinterested at the moment—can see how the overall design should operate, learn how the vineyard is to be pruned and nourished, and demonstrate that the harvest is worth special care.

Along with our God-ordained mission to establish Zion, there are many practical considerations for building strong families. Experience demonstrates that personal happiness is closely tied to the quality of one's marriage and family relations. When a marriage flounders, or when one or more of the children are not living up to gospel standards, a couple feels horrible feelings of failure. We simply cannot be happy if this most important area of our lives is not working well, regardless of what other acclaim may be ours.

Single Parents

Many single parents go it alone. Some even make the difficult trek back to school to update their employment skills, hoping to support themselves and their children. These former spouses often relate a tragic tale of a marriage that didn't work, of the decision to split up, of the anguish, the tears, and finally the resolve to go it alone. (It is interesting to note, however, that even after couples divorce they still must communicate over visitation rights, children's schooling, braces, camp, clothing, finances, and other matters. It makes a person wonder why they didn't stay together in the first place and save all of the hassle! Admittedly, some do communicate better with each other *after* the divorce than before. But why? What caused the change?)

Divorce should be an aberration among this people, reserved only for those who are in marriage and family situations that are intolerable, hopelessly suffocating, and damaging to the persons' spirituality and sanity. There *are* justifiable reasons to dissolve a marriage, and sometimes I see those who should divorce but think the Church does not allow for such situations. In contrast, some who divorce have no business separating under the trivial events and circumstances that bring them to that course of action.

One reason divorce is so contrary to the gospel ideal is that it can hamper or delay exaltation. Exaltation is open only to couples who love and cherish each other and who can build a oneness that deserves an eternal opportunity.

Divorce shatters not only adult lives but also the world of children, who need two healthy parents if they are to be healthy themselves. Children in single-parent families, for example, are six times more likely than children in two-parent families to grow up in an environment of poverty; two to three times more likely to have emotional and behavioral problems; more likely to drop out of school and be expelled or suspended from school; more likely to impregnate someone or become pregnant as a teen; and more likely to use drugs and to become lawbreakers.

Furthermore, family research indicates that many children do not bounce back after divorce, even if their parents remarry. Personality deficiencies and psychological trauma often stem from homes where parents themselves are not healthy and do not model well male and female roles and strong character traits. Youth from such homes are often stunted in their social and moral development. Personality aberrations have a way of persisting into adulthood and becoming the root of abnormal behavior, mental illness, or a variety of character disorders. In addition, such children often have difficulty achieving intimacy in their own adult relationships, in parenting their own children, and in holding a steady job. (Of course, personality disorders may result from factors other than poor parenting models. Accidents, biological imperatives, or psychological trauma of various kinds may impinge on healthy psyches.)

Rebellious Children

Among Latter-day Saint teenagers there are some who break the hearts of faithful parents by rebelling against family and gospel standards, a circumstance due in large part to the ease and softness of modern living, especially in many areas of the United States. Too many youth have too much time on their hands, too much freedom, and too much money to spend. Such blessings as time and means can become curses if they are not used properly. The Book of Mormon warns us that pride is sown "because of . . . prosperity in the land" (Helaman 3:36).

Parents whose children grow up in a city, for example, without many chores to develop discipline and backbone, must find alternate ways to develop work habits in their families. (A mission president's scourge is to have young men and women unwilling or unable to carry out a day's labor.) It seems that without sprinkler pipe to haul, cows to milk, deserts to conquer, land to cultivate, and animals to water and feed, children see little need to get out of their city beds until the sun is well up from the horizon. These kids argue, "What is there to do at that time of day?" And you have to agree that vacuuming floors or mowing lawns or even taking out the garbage are not daily tasks, and they certainly don't need to be done at 6 A.M. If the children watch television until the wee hours the night before, there is even less incentive for them to be early risers. (I hope you will have more parental sense than to let your teens or preteens have their own TV, especially cable, or a VCR in the bedroom.) City parents learn that creativity and ingenuity are required on their part to develop in their children a work ethic. Early-morning scripture study, breakfast together, paper routes, joint work projects and service opportunities are not bad for starters.

The danger is that character traits developed through a life of ease carry over into marriage. One who has been spoiled by parental indulgence will find the demands of marriage a major shock. Children of affluence, whose lives often consist of almost constant entertainment and whose appetites are usually satisfied on demand, will find a rude awakening in marriage, where self-discipline and sacrifice are critical (as when there is a crying newborn at 2 A.M., for example). Like seagulls fed on tourist crackers and bread crumbs who consequently become less independent and responsible, children who have been indulged may lack commitment and courage to stick to marriage when things don't go their way, when individual effort is needed. They will lack the resolve to deal with challenges inherent in forging strong families.

"The trials through which today's young people are passing—ease and luxury—may be the most severe test of any age" cautioned President A. Theodore Tuttle years ago ("The Things That Matter Most," *Ensign,* December 1971, p. 90). President Brigham Young sounded the warning over a century ago: "The worst fear I have about this people is that they will get rich in this country, forget God and His people, wax fat, and kick themselves out of the Church and go to hell. This people will stand mobbing, robbing, poverty and all manner of persecution and be true. But my greatest fear is that they cannot stand wealth." (Quoted in Ezra Taft Benson, *Our Obligation and Challenge,* [Address delivered at Regional Representatives' seminar, 30 September 1977], p. 2.)

Church Inactivity

With the breakup of families, too often comes inactivity in the Church. "After all," many who thus fall into inactivity falsely reason, "if my temple marriage has failed, maybe there is something wrong with the Church." A frantic search for happiness leads some down the wrong paths, while others are swallowed up financially in trying to cope with basic needs of food, clothing, and shelter. Others allow feelings of guilt and unworthiness to drive them away from full Church activity. As singles they become self-conscious and don't feel accepted by other members. Worldly attractions and competing alternatives divert them from gospel standards. Occasionally singles blame the Lord for their predicament. "Why would God allow this to happen to me," they ask, "when I have been active all of my life? I never touched a cigarette, drank, or was immoral in my youth, and look what it got me." They wrongly conclude that the Lord is responsible for their present condition, and their faith is severely tried. Sad to say, many turn their backs just when they need gospel principles and spiritual blessings the most. Little do they know that God weeps along with them at the unwise use his children make of agency (see Moses 7:32–33).

Mark had prayed all his life that the Lord would lead him to marry a virtuous woman who had not been involved in any immorality. He prayed every night of his life, including during his mission years, that the Lord would bless him with a companion who was as "worthy" as he was. He married a beautiful young woman, who confided in him during their honeymoon that she had been careless in an earlier dating experience to the extent of light petting on one occasion. Mark was devastated. He could not bring himself to believe that the Lord would allow him to fall in love with one who had made such a mistake. He spiritually fell apart and ended up divorcing this special young lady, who had repented of her mistake long before the marriage. Mark became inactive in the Church, unable to grasp the power and extent of the Atonement he had taught others about for two years as a missionary.

The Value of the Gospel in Family Relations

Perhaps because I enjoy marriage so much and am awed by the honor and privilege of fatherhood, it is painful for me to watch others, often friends or relatives, who are no longer committed to the spouse to whom they pledged themselves years (sometimes only months!) before. So many seem to struggle so hard to find happiness in the most significant human relationships they form in mortality.

On the positive side, if anyone should be able to do well in marriage and parenting in these challenging times, we, as members of the restored Church, should, for who else understands the eternal plan as we do? Who else knows that we left our premortal life to come to this earth to marry (if we can), to bear children (if we can), and to organize an eternal kingdom? Who else comprehends the eternal potential of the relationship between two spouses and the relationship between parents and their children? Who else knows that marriage is a requirement for exaltation and constitutes a portion of godhood?

The gospel is deeply marriage- and family-oriented, placing us squarely in the family-relations business. The sequence goes something like this: We are born into and grow up in a family, we leave father and mother to organize a family of our own, and we bear and rear children who will repeat the same cycle. Our lives are centered in family life. Will not God hold us accountable for our performances in these important stewardships?

"We shall all be judged and held accountable for how we carry out our various Church assignments," said President Spencer W. Kimball, "and our mortal stewardship will get no more searching scrutiny than with regard to the way we have served and loved our families" ("Our Sisters in the Church," *Ensign,* November 1979, p. 49). And, oh, how rewarding these relationships are as we receive love from and return love to family members and contribute to our mutual well-being! What institution has more impact on our lives than the family? Where else could we invest time and effort to attain the level of happiness that is possible through an intimate companionship and the joy in posterity? No wonder heaven is an extension of our earthly homes.

The doctrine of eternal marriage and family relationships is unique to our Latter-day Saint faith. The exciting message of the Restoration is that physical death and spiritual death have been overcome by the infinite atonement and resurrection of the Son of God. This great gift opens the way for us to continue family associations beyond this life through our resurrection to male and female bodies. What thrilling news to every married couple who love each other and who enjoy children and grandchildren! As his children we can return to our Father in Heaven whole and yet remain an eternal part of our earthly family kingdom. For the faithful, disease and physical ailments that cut short mortal life cannot overpower family ties, for those ties are beyond death's reach.

When families prosper, society is strengthened and God's grand design of bringing to pass "the immortality and eternal life of man" moves forward (see Moses 1:39). The doctrines of the gospel provide an eternal perspective and an incentive to live righteously and to seek exaltation by overcoming and transcending mortality's tests. To know that marriages do not end simply because we die stirs in our souls strong gratitude to Heavenly Father for instituting the plan of salvation and unbounded appreciation for Jesus Christ, who made the plan operational and infinite. No wonder we are Christians. Such love for him becomes a powerful incentive to worship him and not disappoint him; we are motivated to be our best husband and wife selves and to become effective fathers and mothers. People with this perspective stay together through thick and thin. They don't quit at the first sign of trouble or even at a variety of marital differences. Their mutual commitment encourages them to monitor their own actions for the family's good. Applying gospel principles of charity, kindness, long-suffering, patience, meekness, repentance, and forgiveness in family relations becomes the key to success in this great adventure.

Consider what a terrible hoax this life would be if a capricious and unjust God had inaugurated a different plan of salvation. Suppose we were sent to this earth, commanded to marry, directed to "multiply and replenish the earth," only to learn at a later time that it was all a game, for God's curiosity really—his personal experimental laboratory or playground! What if death brought annihilation, or—even worse—what if resurrected beings were neither male nor female? Can you think of a fate more terrible than to be separated forever from a companion of fifty to sixty wonderful years together? If there were no possibility of continuing this relationship, certainly this life would be a profound waste of time and effort on the part of both God and us. Had *that* plan been presented in the premortal council, perhaps more individuals would have adopted the one of our present adversary. A world without the potential of eternal family relations would reduce men and women to the animal level. Certainly morality would have little meaning. We see the results of that philosophy played out in contemporary movies, videos, and books produced by those with no knowledge of our divine potential. Much of what we see on the screen and printed page is offensive to the Spirit and the purposes of God, and decent men and women everywhere are shocked that our society could have sunk so low.

The thesis of Babylon is: "We live for this life only. Seek pleasure for pleasure's sake." This perspective allows people to follow their fallen, carnal natures and justify the "alternative lifestyles" we see in our day. Too many respond to the mating instinct but are unwilling to accept the commitment and responsibilities of marriage, claiming that its arrangement has no relevance to their situation. This lack of an eternal viewpoint has led to an "eat, drink, and be merry, for tomorrow we die," "do your own thing" philosophy that exacts a spiritual toll by its destructive message and consequences.

The restoration of the gospel of Jesus Christ boldly declares that God is not the author of a one-act play about family relations that ends in death. Restoration principles not only stress that families can be forever but also provide the incentive for us to live so that we might attain our highest potential—exaltation. We can establish deep and loving relationships with a spouse and children in this mortal probation because life continues into eternity. Is it not true, then, that these principles commit us to regard marriage and child-rearing as one of our most important earthly priorities?

The Lord explained the reason for the earth's creation: "Verily I say unto you, that whoso forbiddeth to marry is not ordained of God, for marriage is ordained of God unto man. . . . They twain shall be one flesh, and all this [the opportunity to marry] that the earth might answer the end of its creation; and that it might be filled with the measure of man, according to his creation before the world was made." (D&C 49:15–17.)

Summary

We came to this earth to participate in the challenging adventure of family life. With the plan of salvation to guide us, we should have more than a casual interest in wise dating, courtship and marriage, and parenting, for these point to relationships and principles that are the essence of life. Understanding God's grand design will strengthen us in our obedience to marriage covenants and inspire within us the will to be Christlike in our treatment of each other.

CHAPTER TWO

Family Life in Today's World— Our Challenge

Recent years have brought an abundance of bad press concerning the family. Much of it is true, unfortunately, although some of it seems to be a deliberate attempt by evil and "conspiring men" to encourage and justify permissiveness.

Nonetheless, some statistics are shocking: Divorce rates have risen dramatically in past decades, and only recently has the rate leveled off and begun a downturn. It appears that many people are coming to realize that divorce is not much of a solution after all (for example, see Diane Medved, *The Case Against Divorce* [New York: Ivy Books, 1989]). It is a sad commentary on life in the United States that it leads the modern world in the breakup of marriages. Nearly 30 percent of all families in the United States are currently headed by a single parent. The number of people living together without marriage is on the upswing. In many areas, both in and out of the United States, missionaries must insist on marriage for live-in couples before they can be baptized. Abortions are a national disgrace, with more infant bodies destroyed in a single year by medical procedures than the total number of American war dead since our birth as a nation. AIDS is at epidemic levels, threatening innocent people and newborns, and has now become the number one cause of death in many states and cities in the United States.

The definition of *family* has been questioned in our day as gays and lesbians challenge traditional definitions and clamor, absurdly, for homosexual marriages to carry what should be the honorable title of "family." Moreover, the media parade filth *ad nauseam*—themes of adultery, wife and child abuse and neglect, immorality, seduction, and promiscuity. Unfortunately, most script writers are of the opinion that marital stability and fidelity do not offer the same interest, excitement, and appeal to viewers as premarital sex, broken marriages, and infidelity. Often not shown in these movies and programs, however, are the heartache, broken lives, shattered dreams, lost personal worth and esteem, disease, guilt, and disappointment that such immoral actions bring in real life. Such tragedies are witnessed by counselors and church leaders who labor to restore dignity and meaning to individual lives—often with mixed results, at best.

These disturbances are shocking but should not be disheartening to Latter-day Saints; the Lord, through his prophets, has not only warned us of these aberrational trends but also prepared meaningful and practical defenses against them. At first glance these defenses might seem too basic, too simple to the sophisticated. At times we are like our Israelite counterparts of old. Recall that the people of Moses would not be healed from the bite of fiery flying serpents, even though all they had to do was to gaze at the brass serpent on Moses' staff. It was a sure cure, but they would not look up, and "because of the simpleness of the way, or the easiness of it, there were many who perished." (1 Nephi 17:41; see also Numbers 21:6–9.) In another classic example, placing a little lamb's blood over the "lintel and the two side posts" of one's door the night the angel of death swept through Egypt might have seemed unsophisticated to the proud in Moses' day. In this case, however, the children of Israel were all obedient, and at midnight their obedience saved the lives of all their firstborn. (See Exodus 12:21–29.)

In our day, we sometimes behave like those who would not look at the brass serpent; in our supposed sophistication we fail to apply gospel principles in our relationships with others and refuse the assistance available from God's scriptures and latter-day prophets. We ignore the maxim about an ounce of prevention being worth a pound of cure, and like Judah of old, in our stubbornness we begin to look "beyond the mark" (Jacob 4:14).

AIDS illustrates the hardened hearts of our generation. Chastity among the unmarried, fidelity in marriage, and the cessation of drug addiction could wipe out AIDS in a generation—or at least dramatically curtail its spread. Why won't we, as a society, make the necessary commitments? You may answer.

As Latter-day Saints we have been forewarned that attacks against the family were coming, and we have heard the counsel to fortify our homes and children against the coming onslaught. Prophets, as "watchmen on the tower," have given us instruction on temporal and spiritual solutions to preserve our marriages and strengthen our family life. Surely we have been "instructed sufficiently [to] know good from evil" in these matters (see 2 Nephi 2:5). In most cases our problem is not a lack of knowledge or ignorance; it is that we trust in the arm of flesh. We fail to practice what we preach, to do what we know ought to be done. We sometimes seek answers in little more than tabloid literature and embrace telestial and terrestrial answers to spiritual problems.

In 1965 the Church reinstituted family home evening in an effort to strengthen families (the practice of holding home evenings had been introduced in 1915, but the program received renewed attention in this year of 1965). With hindsight, we can now see that this action came as a warning just before the assault against family values began with the hippie movement in the late sixties and early seventies, which made casual sex, drugs, hard-rock music, and sloppy attire popular. Alternative lifestyles were espoused by those who became, unfortunately, the nation's role models for pampered youth. The prophets pleaded with us to gather our families together at least one night each week (Monday evening was designated Church-wide in 1970) so that Church members could reinforce their little brood against the rising tide of filth. Not a fad or temporary swing of the pendulum, this was to be a cultural revolution. In October 1971 general conference, President A. Theodore Tuttle observed:

The world is full of foolish schemes. They contravene and hinder the purposes of the Lord. Some seek to change the God-given roles of the sexes. Some invite mothers to leave the home to work. Others entice fathers to find recreation away from their families. . . .

. . . In a society that tolerates divorce as the inevitable result of 50 percent of its marriages, there is great difficulty transmitting the principle of family solidarity. Children from broken homes seldom carry the idea that the family is an adequate problem-solving organization. Children whose entertainment comes largely from television find their needs for involvement in life frequently frustrated. Where a doctor who stops at the scene of an accident may be sued for administering aid, it is difficult to transmit to children the idea of service and responsibility.

In a home where the accumulation of worldly goods has become so important that the father works inordinately at providing financial security at the expense of spending time with his children and sharing his counsel and encouragement; and in a home, likewise, where the mother forsakes her children in order to get more "things," it is a poor place to teach the worth of a human being in terms of love and sacrifice. ("The Things That Matter Most," *Ensign,* December 1971, pp. 90, 91.)

Elsewhere in this talk, President Tuttle counseled: "The failure of fathers and mothers to assume their rightful responsibilities actually creates the disturbed conditions we face. As Latter-day Saints, we must resist the 'thrust of the world' against our homes. Repentance is in order for many of us. We *must* put our values in proper perspective. Put time and attention and means on the things that matter most. Few, in their more sober moments of reflection, do not know where true values rest." ("The Things That Matter Most," p. 91.)

External Influences

A number of destructive movements against and inroads into decency that had an impact on marriage and family relations began shortly after the Church's 1965 introduction of the family home evening program. James C. Dobson (though not a Latter-day Saint), in a May 1993 letter to *Focus on the Family* readers, identified a number of events, characters, and ideas that played a role in bringing about so many radical changes in our social fabric, pinpointing 1968 as being a particularly impactful year. Excerpts from his discussion follow:

> *Newsweek* said, "The year 1968 will not be remembered as a gentle one. Like the rebellious youths whom it spawned in such abundance, the year's unruly brood of surprises tore into the public tranquility with an apparent vengeance. At times, under 1968's hammer blows, it seemed almost routine for traditions to be upset, expectations jarred, proprieties offended, the frontiers of man's experience pushed outward, and the hopes or even lives of prominent men cut abruptly short." ["That Was the Year That Was," Newsweek, January 6, 1969, p. 3.]
>
> Although I doubt if anyone living through those days has forgotten them, let me cite a few of the tragic events punctuating that year of dramatic *change:* . . .
>
> • On April 4, Dr. Martin Luther King was killed by James Earl Ray in Memphis, Tenn. His murder sent shock waves throughout the United States, setting off riots in numerous cities.
>
> • On June 5, Sen. Robert Kennedy was murdered by Sirhan Bishara Sirhan at the Ambassador Hotel in Los Angeles. Americans staggered in disbelief as another of their public personalities, and the second Kennedy, fell victim to an assassin's bullet. . . .
>
> • In one of the most regrettable episodes in American political history, the Democratic National Convention was disrupted by bloody student riots involving thousands of students on the streets of Chicago. More than 100 protesters were injured as police intercepted a planned march to the International Amphitheater four miles away. Millions of Americans witnessed the rebellion on television and wondered what else could go wrong in their beleaguered nation.
>
> These acts of violence did not occur in a vacuum. They were symptomatic of a larger phenomena—a spirit of anarchy that prevailed through 1968 in various parts of the world. . . .
>
> In the United States, this defiance had begun nonviolently in 1967 during the infamous "Summer of Love." Millions of young people took to the streets in pursuit of free love, free speech and free drugs. They seemed to be having such a good time at first, as words like "far-out," "groovy," "flower power," "be-in," "mellow," "trip," "cool," "uptight," "outta sight," "peace" and "relevant" became shibboleths of the age.

But by 1968, things started turning nasty. Anger began to seethe within those of college age. Hatred for the government, its leaders, its institutions and its values oozed from the pores of this movement. Concepts of morality and common sense that had undergirded society for centuries suddenly became old-fashioned, oppressive and obscene. Behavior that had been almost unthinkable became avant-garde and chic. The world held its breath as revolutionary changes swept through society—to the utter delight of the media.

The Beatles rock group played a key role in this rebellion. John Lennon, an outspoken atheist, had stunned the religious community in 1966 by saying, "Christianity will go. It will vanish and shrink. I needn't argue about that. I'm right and I will be proved right. We're more popular than Jesus now; I don't know which will go first—rock'n roll or Christianity. Jesus was all right, but his disciples were thick and ordinary. It's them twisting it that ruins it for me"! ["According to John," *Time*, August 12, 1966, p. 38.] . . .

Jack Weinberg, one of the movement leaders, advised the younger generation not to trust anyone over 30 years of age. . . .

. . . Even now, 25 years later, we are still suffering from some of the excesses of those days. . . . Only by examining the turmoil of our past can we understand ourselves and the world in which we live. . . .

Many of our most serious social problems can be traced directly to five bad ideas that gained popular acceptance in the late '60s. They continue to plague us today.

1. Drug usage makes great recreational sport, especially when you are young.

Dr. Timothy Leary advised teenagers and college students to "turn on, tune in and drop out" [Edward P. Morgan, *The '60s Experience: Hard Lessons About Modern America* (Philadelphia: Temple University Press, 1991), p. 197]. He also advised them that the "fifth freedom" was "the right to get high." Allen Ginsberg told a group assembled at a Boston church in 1966 that everyone over the age of 14 ought to try LSD at least once. The Beatles promoted LSD and marijuana as the ultimate (Eastern) religious experience. Their recording "Sergeant Pepper's Lonely Hearts Club Band" was a poorly disguised promotion of the drug experience.

A bleary-eyed generation responded enthusiastically. In August 1969, 400,000 young people flocked to Woodstock for three days of drugs, sex and rock and roll. Haight-Ashbury in San

Francisco became the permanent "crash pad" for runaways and burned-out revolutionaries. . . .

In 1969, the Rolling Stones hired some Hell's Angels to provide security for a concert at Altamont Speedway in Northern California. In full view of the stage, they stabbed to death a black concertgoer and beat up many others.

Death then claimed a number of popular rock musicians, including:

• Brian Jones (of the Rolling Stones), who died of a drug overdose, July 5, 1969.

• Jimi Hendrix, who died of a heroin overdose, Sept. 18, 1970.

• Janis Joplin, who died of a heroin overdose, Oct. 4, 1970.

• Jim Morrison, who died of a drug overdose, July 3, 1971.

There were more—thousands more—who fried their brains and wracked their bodies with illegal substances. Some of their children are making the same tragic mistake today. . . .

The National Organization for the Reform of Marijuana Laws (NORML) has counted 45 rock groups that have declared their support for legalized pot ["High Times Return: Pot Makes a Comeback Among Musicians," *USA Today*, March 19, 1993, p. 2D]. . . .

2. Premarital, extramarital and perverted sex are moral and healthy if done "properly" and with mutual consent.

The sexual revolution blew in like a tornado and swept away all the old prohibitions and fears. The pill prevented pregnancy and antibiotics eliminated disease. So what possible reason was left to preserve virginity? "Coupling" came out of the bedroom and into everyday conversation. "Why don't we do it in the road?" sang the Beatles. "Hello, I love you, won't you tell me your name?" wailed the Doors. "Make love, not war," read the bumper stickers. . . . They called their extravaganza the "new morality," which was neither new nor moral. But they certainly appeared to be having fun.

Who would have thought that such excitement would produce the disease and misery we face today? Who could have envisioned the AIDS phenomenon that may eventually kill 100 million people, or the 20 other sexually transmitted diseases that have infected the human family? Who would have expected syphilis and gonorrhea to get completely out of control, or that by 1993, more than 43 million Americans would suffer from incurable, sexually transmitted viruses? Who would have believed that 27 million unborn babies would have been aborted, or that infertility would plague one out of five married couples? . . .

3. Radical feminism offers the only justice and equality for women.

Gloria Steinem wrote, "A woman needs a man like a fish needs a bicycle" [Sally Quinn, "Feminists Have Killed Feminism," *Los Angeles Times,* January 23, 1992]. Then she denounced marriage as a form of prostitution [Peter Collier and David Horowitz, *Deconstructing the Left: From Vietnam to the Persian Gulf,* (Lanham, Md.: Second Thoughts Books and Center for the Study of Popular Culture, 1991), p. 18]. Kate Millett delivered a short manifesto called "Sexual Politics" to a women's liberation meeting at Cornell, which for the first time characterized men and women as political enemies [Michele Ingrassia, "NOW and Then: A Look at the Origins of Feminism," *Newsday,* October 29, 1991]. . . .

. . . Feminist ideology brought to light many legitimate concerns that needed to be addressed, and some positive consequences have resulted. But the radical members of the movement were (and are) committed to a godless agenda, including abortion-on-demand, lesbian rights, and hostility to men. . . .

4. God is dead. May He rest in peace.

On April 8, 1966, *Time* devoted its cover story to the question "Is God dead?" ["Is God Dead?" *Time,* April 8, 1966, p. 82.] . . . By casting doubt on God's existence and preeminence, society was cut loose from scriptural moorings and historic restraints. Thereafter, "each man did what was right in his own eyes" (Judges 17:6). . . .

5. Divorce is an easy way out for the frustrated, disappointed or adventuresome.

Mel Krantzler wrote a book entitled *Creative Divorce,* in which he stated: "To say goodbye is to say hello . . . hello to a new life— to a new, freer, more self-assured you. Hello to new ways of looking at the world and of relating to people. Your divorce can turn out to be the very best thing that ever happened to you!" [*Creative Divorce: A New Opportunity for Personal Growth,* (New York: M. Evans and Company Inc., 1973).] That was a widely held professional opinion for almost a decade. To many, it seemed like a good idea at the time.

When buttressed by "no fault" divorce laws that weakened the ties that bind, the number of disintegrating families went through the roof. A spate of pseudo-scientific studies assured parents that children were resilient and would recover quickly from the effects of divorce. Whether they suffered or not, however, a person had to do what a person had to do. "I gotta be me," sang Sammy Davis Jr., reflecting the mood of the times. "I did it my way," warbled

Frank Sinatra. The number-one best-seller was *Looking Out for Number One* by Robert J. Ringer. The common wisdom of the day was to "Do your own thing," and "If it feels good, do it." Selfishness was definitely in style, and it took its toll on family stability. (James C. Dobson, letter to subscribers, *Focus on the Family,* May 1993, pp. 1–5; used with permission.)

If you are over forty, you are a witness to these events that transformed society in radical ways that continue into the mid-nineties and beyond.

President Spencer W. Kimball confirmed that a preoccupation with self, or selfishness, was the principal cause of marital instability:

> Every divorce is the result of selfishness on the part of one or the other or both parties to a marriage contract. Someone is thinking of self—comforts, conveniences, freedoms, luxuries, or ease. Sometimes the ceaseless pinpricking of an unhappy, discontented, and selfish spouse can finally add up to serious physical violence. Sometimes people are goaded to the point where they erringly feel justified in doing the things which are so wrong. Nothing, of course, justifies sin. ("Marriage and Divorce," in *1976 Devotional Speeches of the Year* [Provo, Utah: Brigham Young University Press, 1977], p. 148.)

To counter these social trends, Church leaders commissioned a series of family home evening manuals containing lessons and teaching helps for every family to combat numerous latter-day heresies. These materials were geared to every family regardless of the ages or the number of children and were available free of charge. In fact, many not of the Latter-day Saint faith complimented the Church's bold move and either asked for permission to use the materials directly or imitated them. As a follow-up, in 1985 the Church published a *Family Home Evening Resource Book* with further helps to maintain close family ties. My own unofficial observations indicate that less than half of the members of the Church actually used these resources, a situation reminiscent of the brass-serpent episode in Moses' day. Subsequently, President Ezra Taft Benson counseled us to read the Book of Mormon and the Doctrine and Covenants to supplement our home evening program.

Since the end of the 1960s, the offensive made against the family by secular cynics, militant feminists, gays, lesbians, and a parade of other antifamily advocates has spawned a host of secular doctrines that could seriously undermine the family. Consider, for example, how commonly we hear of people living together without ever getting married, or of pregnant teens who do not marry and who, once their babies are born, keep them and raise them alone or with parents. Think how brazen movies have become in depicting immodesty and explicit sexual themes. Does not our society reek with decadence?

Many of these external challenges to family unity have come with our increased standard of living and technological and scientific progress, which have improved creature comforts and freed us to concentrate on our own selfish gain. The result has been a major preoccupation with self, as President Kimball warned. Our culture has been turned upside down by modern trends. In a college text on marriage and family, Carlfred B. Broderick observed:

> Since the turn of the century, courtship and marriage have been reshaped by the automobile, the telephone, the movies, the media, the development of reliable contraceptives, frozen foods, microwave ovens, plastic wrap, refrigerators, television, central heating, super highways, jet travel, and pollution. The social changes have been at least as dramatic. Two world wars and two "police actions," the Great Depression, stagflation, immigration, population explosion, the decay of the cities, the migration from the farm, and the growth of the suburbs have all had an irreversible impact, as has the civil rights movement, the student revolt of the 1960s, and the women's movement. (*Marriage and the Family* [Englewood Cliffs, N. J.: Prentice-Hall, 1979], p. 10.)

Historically, few societies have survived the blessings and curses of prosperity. It is estimated that the average American watches between five and seven hours of television per day, which allows wickedness to be transmitted in greater abundance than ever before! Improved technology and Madison Avenue marketing have fanned our demand for more and more goods and services. The danger of this, we should remember from the Book of Mormon, is that people who seek material goals turn from ideals to idols, from dependence on God to dependence on self and others, including government. We begin to think that the source of happiness is money (especially when it is gained through winning the lotto), wealth, gadgets, education, and asset accumulation rather than personal righteousness, close families ties, and service to others.

Are we not reliving the Book of Mormon experience that Moroni warned us about? (See Ether 2:11.) When the Nephites were confronted with political freedom, economic prosperity, leisure time, and consumer goods, they cast off their spiritual anchor—Christ. They grew indifferent and even hostile to the counsel of their prophets. Prosperity overwhelmed them. (See Helaman 3:33–36; 12:1–4.) Similarly, seeking goods and gadgets distracts many of us and begins to take precedence over spiritual goals. We live in the most prosperous time in world history, yet we suffer much misery due to family instability. Our test of opulence is one that few societies have survived without the family's becoming a major casualty.

An incident from the Book of Mormon teaches a message of relevance for our day. On one occasion a group of "have nots" were cast out of their synagogues because of poverty and low social status. Alma counseled these people that this could be a blessing *if* they learned from it:

> I say unto you, it is well that ye are cast out of your synagogues, that ye may be humble, and that ye may learn wisdom; for it is necessary that ye should learn wisdom. . . .
>
> And now, because ye are compelled to be humble blessed are ye; for a man sometimes, if he is compelled to be humble, seeketh repentance; and now surely, whosoever repenteth shall find mercy; and he that findeth mercy and endureth to the end the same shall be saved.
>
> And now, as I said unto you, that because ye were compelled to be humble ye were blessed, do ye not suppose that they are more blessed who truly humble themselves because of the word?
>
> Yea, he that truly humbleth himself, and repenteth of his sins, and endureth to the end, the same shall be blessed—yea, much more blessed than they who are compelled to be humble because of their exceeding poverty.
>
> Therefore, blessed are they who humble themselves without being compelled to be humble. (Alma 32:12–16.)

As Latter-day Saints in times of relative peace and prosperity, instead of succumbing to the temptation to increase our lands and possessions, we must take advantage of the period in between wars, while men are home instead of at war, to strengthen our families and bind us together through principles that safeguard family values. Instead of fighting in foreign lands, defending our liberties, we can concentrate on being fathers. We can focus on spiritual objectives and not be lulled into a chase of worldly praise and honor. "Why do ye adorn yourselves with that which hath no life," Moroni asked, "and yet suffer the hungry, and the needy, and the naked, and the sick and the afflicted to pass by you, and notice them not?" (Mormon 8:39.) Sometimes the needy, the naked, and the spiritually starved are members of our own household. We must not neglect our own family members. (See the entire chapter of Mormon 8.)

We are called to be the Lord's standard-bearers, the salt of the earth. We must point out the path and be examples of righteousness for the world to follow. "And, now, behold, if Zion do these things," the Lord explained in 1833, referring to the building of a temple, among other things, "she shall prosper. . . . And the nations of the earth shall honor her, and shall say: Surely Zion is the city of our God, and surely Zion cannot fall, neither be moved out of her place, for God is there, and the hand of the Lord is there." (D&C 97:18–19.) It has turned out to be prophetic that President Spencer W. Kimball could say in 1974 that "every young man" should serve a mission. Before that time, wars and other circumstances had prevented some young men from being able to participate. We have now had, at least those from the United States, twenty years of virtually uninterrupted opportunity to take the gospel to the world without the encumbrances that war and conflict bring. (See "When the World Will Be Converted," *Ensign,* October 1974, pp. 2–14.)

Internal Influences

The other challenge to marital stability comes from inside the family itself. By the time most couples come to Church or family counselors and pour out their grief and emotions, the problems have grown more complicated. These practitioners do not have miracle medicines or injections that bring dramatic results. Impaired relationships do not yield to the scalpel, antibiotics, or wonder drugs. They do, however, yield to a change of heart, to repentance, to godly sorrow, to a broken heart and contrite spirit. But in our day of selfishness and materialism, such attitude changes are very difficult to initiate without a crisis of sufficient magnitude to humble the human spirit (see Helaman 12:1–4).

We need to return to basic gospel principles; moreover, we need to strengthen our doctrinal and theological moorings. We must constantly nourish the vision of a healthy family as the basic element of a stable community. Marriages must provide positive role models for children, who in turn can come to know by precept and example that Christ and his gospel provide the only sane ways to traverse the quagmire of mortality.

Selfishness destroys marriage and family relations. Those who marry young (or imitate marriage by moving in together) are usually seeking to achieve their own selfish ends, to mimic marriage, or to escape from a disturbed home environment. Such youth want to partake of the privileges of marriage without the emotional and spiritual preparation necessary to succeed in organizing and running a family enterprise. The teenage period, particularly ages fourteen through nineteen, can be a very self-centered time of life. It is a time of dating, driving, first employment, and money. As teens earn income, there are multitudes of items to exchange for their paychecks—fashions, jewelry, cars, stereos, travel, video games, gadgets—as well as possible opportunities for travel. These symbols of affluence can become the driving force behind perceived status and a desire to acquire more possessions. Acquisitions and popularity become more important than missions or service. Self-esteem is then gauged by possessions and by the latest in clothing and hairstyles. But prosperity combined with a "do your own thing" philosophy brings the old Nephite diseases of pride, rebellion against authority, immorality, arrogance, temper, and defensiveness.

Much of what passes for humor in modern television sitcoms is based on put-downs, sarcastic replies, disrespect for traditions, and seductive themes, which are then dumped into our homes like raw sewage unless we are wise enough to stop or avoid them. If we don't check our viewing habits, we may find ourselves and our children repeating the language and vulgar comments of these culture heroes. Although such verbal broadsides might appear sophisticated and clever, the resulting casualties that can occur in real life are disrupted relationships, lowered self-esteem, and poor modeling for family relations. Venting negative and disrespectful comments to each other impairs the family unit and deals family solidarity a severe blow.

Statistics prove that youth under age twenty generally are ill-prepared for the demands of marriage. During these early dating years both sexes are usually anxious to be cool and emotionally detached. We tend to hide personality weaknesses from others while dating and display only socially acceptable behavior in public. In addition, particularly when we are young our emotions, fanned by verbal and nonverbal messages from a dating partner, can cause us to mistake sexual intrigue and enticement for love and can thus dull our ability to make sensible, long-term decisions with both head and heart.

Value of Missions

Little wonder that the prophets have counseled young men on the value of a mission, where much-needed maturity, perspective, and unselfish qualities essential to later success in marriage and family life can be learned. Missions help young men and women to avoid many problems that would otherwise cause marital stress, and their having served increases the probability that they will make adjustments in a Christlike manner. Learning how to discuss and apply gospel principles through increased communication skills can only benefit a later marital relationship. Inviting a young man enamored with material trappings to voluntarily enter the mission field, cut his hair, care for and wear only a few well-chosen clothes, all while experiencing frequent rejection for twenty-four months, can bring about the refinement of that young man's character. Missions can make men out of boys and women out of girls.

Missionaries learn gospel principles, leadership, companionship skills, spirituality, fasting and prayer, scripture study, humility, and perspective to a much greater extent than they would have had they remained at home. No wonder Church statistics reflect the fact that returned missionaries are a major strength to the kingdom. In general, they remain committed to the faith. A high percentage of them marry in the temple, their individual lives reflect a personal testimony and commitment to basic principles of obedience, faith, tithing, prayer, and scripture study, and they respond to important callings in ward and stake organizations. Temple marriages have the lowest of all divorce rates.

Without a mission experience, male Church members may struggle with activity because (1) they have had less incentive to study the scriptures, not having been "forced" to explain them to people who do not always accept them; (2) they tend to feel awkward in quorum and Sunday School classes where they are surrounded by returned missionaries with perhaps more experience in understanding gospel principles; (3) they might hesitate to accept callings due to a lack of confidence in speaking or teaching others who they feel know more than they do; (4) sometimes in their inactivity they break basic commandments, causing guilt that prevents or delays their return to activity.

Summary

External and internal challenges confront our families. We must be in the world but not of it. Family home evening, scripture study, consistent and wise parental teaching and supervision, and establishing solid relationships with our children will help us combat the evils of the day as we consistently apply gospel principles. While gospel study and living gospel principles are helpful in developing the personal faith and testimony of anyone who will do them, serving a mission significantly helps prepare young men and women for the roles of husband, wife, father, and mother, as well as for Church service and eventual exaltation.

Handwritten note:

Healthy people / individuals
+ find other healthy people
marry
= healthy children
⇒ bless progress of church

Practices That Strengthen

Marriage and Family Relations

The family is the wellspring from which humanity emerges and enters the social stream. When that wellspring is free of debris and contaminants, individuals come forth who strengthen society. If the source is polluted or obstructed, however, not only do individual personalities suffer but also the families themselves, thus eventually tainting the larger reservoir. Healthy people are able to attract healthy mates, and together they bear and rear children who maintain and often improve the social order. Marriage is the critical relationship in families, for, in general, as the marriage goes, so goes the family. Strong families are critical to the progress of the Church, for the Lord's work is impeded when the Saints struggle in their home life.

The Father ordained the family as the basic unit of his kingdom in this life and the next. Jesus Christ, as the Father's Firstborn in the premortal life and Only Begotten in the flesh, made it possible for us to live forever as resurrected male beings

[handwritten annotation: Be in love now... Why would you want to be eternally together if you don't love each other.]

[handwritten annotation: Married couples have children fast don't know each other, fall apart when children leave, dating didn't happen when children in home]

...fore, that after spend-...ompanions, our great-...death is to continue...In truth, that is the...altation continues this (see D&C 131:1–4)....value if our marriages...were not valuable to us...to think that we could...at after death we would...with each other and anx-...allenge in this life is to...ips so that each family...the others eternally (see D&C 130:2). Before mortality we... never had this privilege to marry and reproduce. This is our first-ever opportunity. And for those who do not gain exaltation, it will be their last (see D&C 131:2–4). As parents, our goal is to strengthen our own marriages and then help our children grow to maturity as well-rounded individuals—stable, capable, and spiritual—so that they can attract a mate, consummate a marriage, and bear and rear children who will fulfill their own missions in life. Priesthood authority makes it possible for an appointed officiator to unite a couple in the sacred temple ordinance of eternal marriage, which will help qualify that couple for exaltation. By covenant with God, the two gain the power to inherit "eternal lives" in the resurrection (see D&C 132:24).

Even though such a marriage begins with a sealing "for time and all eternity," every couple so married has the challenge to blend their strengths in a united effort. To achieve this oneness, each spouse must develop Christlike attributes that will enrich and enhance their relationship. These traits help to make both partners more attractive, lovable, and charitable. When two people marry, they know relatively little about each other, because dating can be somewhat superficial and both of them are usually young and relatively immature. Marriage quickly complicates simple relationships as couples must deal with the demands of earning a living and managing finances, as well as with work and school schedules, intimacy and pregnancy, infants and children, in-laws, and a number of associated issues.

It isn't until two married people live day in and day out with each other and with children that we come to know each other's heart and soul and begin to catch a glimpse of the real meaning of love.

The Key to Marital Stability and Exaltation

The key to succeeding in marriage so as to attain exaltation is to understand the doctrines of the gospel regarding marriage and family and thereby gain a standard to guide our lives. Elder Boyd K. Packer explained the connection between doctrine and behavior: "The study of the doctrines of the gospel will improve behavior quicker than a study of behavior will improve behavior. . . . That is why we stress so forcefully the study of the doctrines of the gospel." (In Conference Report, October 1986, p. 20.)

Doctrines about marriage and family outline the purpose and potential of these relationships. Knowing that marriage can be eternal encourages us not only to be careful in our mate selection but also to commit ourselves to do all we can to ensure that our marriage succeeds. How we relate to each other, treat each other, and meet each other's needs contributes to our marital happiness and stability.

Elder Neal A. Maxwell made the following connection between the plan of salvation and our happiness:

> One of the great blessings flowing from amplifying, latter-day revelations is the crucial, doctrinal framework known as the marvelous plan of salvation, the plan of happiness, or the plan of mercy. (See Alma 42:5, 8, 15.) However designated, it represents what Amulek called the "great plan of the Eternal God" without which mankind would unavoidably perish. (Alma 34:9.) . . .
>
> So vital is this framework that if one stays or strays outside it, he risks . . . misery. In fact, most human misery represents ignorance of or noncompliance with the plan. A cessation of such mortal suffering will not come without compliance to it. ("The Great Plan of the Eternal God," *Ensign,* May 1984, p. 21.)

When marriage and family relations are tucked in the framework of the plan of salvation, we increase our chances to succeed.

For Latter-day Saints married in the temple, divorce is especially serious because it involves breaking covenants. This not only displeases the Lord but also indicates to God and the divorced person that he or she cannot live according to the very plan God ordained to exalt His children, at least not at that point in the person's life. Of course many find another partner and make new covenants. But at the time of divorce, one or both partners are not living the gospel so as to qualify for exaltation, while the divorce itself, at least temporarily, makes them ineligible for eternal life.

Only married couples are invited into the highest degree of glory; neither man nor woman is whole or complete without a member of the opposite sex. Exaltation is not a solo act. The highest degree of glory is designed for two covenant people who love each other in this life and have an intense desire to continue that relationship beyond this temporary sphere. (See D&C 131:2–4.) Divorce may hinder, delay, or completely prevent exaltation. No wonder those who were responsible for broken marriages were condemned by the Savior (see Matthew 19:9–11). Although divorce may be necessary and justifiable in some cases, those who find themselves in such situations and who get divorced must not allow that divorce to canker their souls or sour them on marriage. Some singles become angry at all members of the opposite sex and thereby damage their own spirituality. We must never lose faith in marriage.

Table 1 illustrates the relationship between doctrine, perspective, covenants, behavior, and exaltation, and shows the practical path to exaltation. It should be emphasized that we cannot be perfected without the atonement of Jesus Christ, nor can we "work" to exaltation, regardless of our righteousness. Grace is necessary to fill the gap between our best efforts and the perfection required for the celestial kingdom. As Nephi said, "It is by grace that we are saved, after all we can do" (2 Nephi 25:23). The Savior met the demands of justice, opening the door for mercy to intervene when we repent. Through the atonement of Christ, grace lifts us to a higher state than we have merited by our own righteousness. Thus, through repentance and Christ's atonement, we can change, improve, and grow in righteousness and in our ability to carry out marital roles more effectively. Then, following the resurrection, our kingdom continues to expand.

Table 1

How Doctrines, Perspective, and Covenants Influence Behavior and Lead Us to Exaltation

When we understand doctrines such as: ------	Then we gain a proper perspective on such matters as: ------	Which leads to our making covenants (or commitments) involving: ------	Which leads to our developing righteous behaviors such as: ------	Which leads to exaltation
The atonement and resurrection of Jesus Christ	Marriage	Promises to God	Christlike treatment of others	Eternal marriage
The premortal life	Husbands' and wives' responsibilities	Promises to a spouse	Loving a spouse	Eternal increase
The purpose of life	Procreation	Promises to live worthy of exaltation	Loving one's children	Godlike nature
The three degrees of glory	Parenthood	Ratification by the Holy Ghost if we are faithful	Forgiving others	Fulness of joy
Satan's damnation	Fidelity		Repenting	Celestial kingdom
All are Heavenly Father's spirit children	Male and female traits		Caring for others	
			Serving others	
			Showing unconditional love	
			Living so as to please God	
			Living so as to become like God	

Doctrines Concerning Marriage
and Family Relations

To apply Elder Packer's point about doctrine and behavior, we might ask what principles have power to generate in us a desire to succeed in marriage because we want to be our best as a marriage partner. I have included a few here: (1) the atonement and resurrection of Jesus Christ, (2) the premortal life, which provides meaning for marriage and family relations, (3) the three degrees of glory, (4) the actual damnation and curse of Lucifer, and (5) the privilege to be the mortal parents of God's spirit children.

The Atonement and Resurrection

It is by virtue of the Savior's atonement and resurrection that we can return to our Heavenly Father as resurrected beings and enjoy all the blessings he has reserved for the faithful, including those of eternal marriage and eternal increase. As Elder Bruce R. McConkie wrote: "Salvation comes because of the atonement. Without it the whole plan of salvation would be frustrated and the whole purpose behind the creating and populating of the earth would come to naught. With it the eternal purposes of the Father will roll forth, the purpose of creation be preserved, the plan of salvation made efficacious, and men will be assured of a hope of the highest exaltation hereafter." (*Mormon Doctrine,* 2d ed. [Salt Lake City: Bookcraft, 1966], p. 61.)

Obtaining the "highest exaltation" means, in part, enjoying the blessings of eternal marriage and an eternal family. Priesthood keys restored by Elias to Joseph Smith allow the organization of eternal families, while the authority restored by Elijah enables couples to be sealed together for time and eternity, so that each couple may qualify for exaltation (see D&C 110: 12–16). The couple's righteousness ensures their worthiness to live with others who have attained the same spiritual stature. "Then shall they be gods," the revelation says, "because they have no end; therefore shall they be from everlasting to everlasting, because they continue" (D&C 132:20).

On 30 June 1916, the First Presidency and the Council of the Twelve Apostles issued a statement that read, in part:

So far as the stages of eternal progression and attainment have been made known through divine revelation, we are to understand that only resurrected and glorified beings can become parents of spirit offspring. Only such exalted souls have reached maturity in the appointed course of eternal life; and the spirits born to them in the eternal worlds will pass in due sequence through the several stages or estates by which the glorified parents have attained exaltation. (In *Messages of the First Presidency,* comp. James R. Clark, 6 vols. [Salt Lake City: Bookcraft, 1965–75], 5:34.)

In this regard, we read in the Doctrine and Covenants: "In the celestial glory there are three heavens or degrees; and in order to obtain the highest, a man must enter into this order of the priesthood [meaning the new and everlasting covenant of marriage]; and if he does not, he cannot obtain it. He may enter into the other, but that is the end of his kingdom; he cannot have an increase." (D&C 131:1–4.)

Elder Melvin J. Ballard explained:

What do we mean by endless or eternal increase? We mean that through the righteousness and faithfulness of men and women who keep the commandments of God they will come forth with celestial bodies, fitted and prepared to enter into their great, high and eternal glory in the celestial kingdom of God; and unto them, through their preparation, there will come spirit children. I don't think that is very difficult to comprehend. The nature of the offspring is determined by the nature of the substance that flows in the veins of the being. When blood flows in the veins of the being the offspring will be what blood produces, which is tangible flesh and bone; but when that which flows in the veins is spirit matter, a substance which is more refined and pure and glorious than blood, the offspring of such beings will be spirit children. (*Melvin J. Ballard: Crusader for Righteousness* [Salt Lake City: Bookcraft, 1966], p. 211.)

When we talk of marriage and family, we touch on eternal things, for we are eternal beings. We touch on the true source of happiness, on the fountain of life, on feelings and emotions. God established that man and woman should not be alone. It is through marriage that we reach our highest potential as males and females, husbands and wives, fathers and mothers.

I have learned that the longer I am married, the more I love my wife and cherish our association. The more we share our feelings and experiences together (often in our early-morning walks), the stronger my love and appreciation for her grow. The more intertwined our lives become through children, finances, and intimacy, as we learn about and meet each other's needs, and as we cope with our mutual aging, the more I care about her and want to be with her forever—not just for a few brief years together here.

When I think of this close association with my wife, I do not think I could worship a God who would design a plan that would have me come to earth, gain my mortal body, marry my sweetheart, rear children, spend all of my mortal years in family relationships, and that then, after all the cherished experiences and emotional affiliations I had gained through those associations, would allow either my wife or me to die and cause us to lose in the grave everything we had done together. If that were the end, I would want nothing to do with Christianity. If the atonement of Jesus Christ did not have the power to bring about the resurrection of us all as well as provide a way for family associations to be eternal, what purpose could Christ's mission have had? Without the assurances that the restored gospel provides, we would live in constant fear that one of our family members might lose his or her life and thus cut short our family associations.

Don't misunderstand me. The perspective we gain through the gospel does help us see beyond the grave; nevertheless, death is still not something we generally look forward to before our time. But without this gospel perspective, if indeed death marked the end of the family life God planned for us, every honest soul would ask, Why would God perpetrate such a hoax? Why would a being who has eternal life within himself, who knows all things, and who has all power implement such a useless and wasteful plan? What is the purpose of it all? Why did we come here? Why marry? And why bear and rear children? As a song of our day says, "If love doesn't last forever, what's forever for?"

I want my association with my wife to last forever, and I have similar feelings about my association with my children. I am deeply involved in their lives, and I want to help them with-

out interfering in their growth and agency. Each of my children is important to me and contributes to my happiness. Is it not my work (and perhaps someday my glory) to bring to pass their eternal life in any way that I can? From my own limited experience with my little kingdom, I know, in some small degree at least, how Heavenly Father must feel about each member of his family.

Elder George Q. Cannon summarized this noble adventure of marriage and family:

> We believe that when a man and woman are united as husband and wife, and they love each other, their hearts and feelings are one, that that love is as enduring as eternity itself, and that when death overtakes them it will neither extinguish nor cool that love, but that it will brighten and kindle it to a purer flame, and that it will endure through eternity; and that if we have offspring they will be with us and our mutual associations will be one of the chief joys of the heaven to which we are hastening. . . . God has restored the everlasting priesthood, by which ties can be formed, consecrated and consummated, which shall be as enduring as we ourselves are enduring, that is, as our spiritual nature; and husbands and wives will be united together, and they and their children will dwell and associate together eternally, and this, as I have said, will constitute one of the chief joys of heaven; and we look forward to it with delightful anticipations. (In *Journal of Discourses* 14:320–21.)

This principle of the eternal nature of the family is one of the great and joyous truths revealed in the present dispensation. Marriage and family life were meant to be eternal, for we ourselves are eternal.

Adam and Eve made mortality and children possible, and Jesus Christ made it possible for marriage to be forever. No wonder we shouted for joy in the premortal realms at the prospect of this earth life (see Job 38:7). Marriage is a wonderful opportunity to plumb the wondrous depths of another soul in an emotional outpouring of feelings and impressions, for a man and wife to share intimately in the miracle of birth, the creation of a soul. What a profound experience for a husband to watch his wife bring forth a child, to bring to earth a spirit son or daughter of God, one who desires this mortal stewardship too. Marriage connects our past eternity as a single person to a future eternity of marriage and family life.

The Premortal Life and the Purpose of Mortality

The premortal life is another doctrine that profoundly influences our perspective and behavior. The principle underlying this doctrine is that we lived in God's presence as his literal offspring before this mortal life. We were spirits, male and female, in form similar to our mortal bodies (see D&C 77:2). However, it appears that a spirit body in the premortal life was incapable of reproduction. One of the primary purposes in our coming to this second estate, therefore, is to obtain a body of flesh and blood that enables us to marry and become stewards over children.

The Lord explained this purpose of the earth's creation: "And again, verily I say unto you, that whoso forbiddeth to marry is not ordained of God, for marriage is ordained of God unto man. Wherefore, . . . they twain shall be one flesh, and all this that the earth might answer the end of its creation; and that it might be filled with the measure of man, according to his creation before the world was made." (D&C 49:15–17.)

The earth was created, in part, as a residence for our spirits while they are housed in mortal tabernacles. Here we grow to adulthood, marry, and become capable of generating life. As mentioned earlier, not one of us ever had the privilege to marry and be a parent before this existence. This is a significant point. Consider how long we anticipated this opportunity.

How long *did* we live in God's presence before our mortal birth, and what were we like in that premortal state? We know that each of us was a single adult, male or female, a son or daughter of God, and that we lived in His presence for a long period. President Brigham Young explained: "You are well acquainted with God our Heavenly Father, or the great Elohim. You are all well acquainted with him, for there is not a soul of you but what has lived in his house and dwelt with him year after year. . . . There is not a person here to-day but what is a son or a daughter of that Being. In the spirit world their spirits were first begotten and brought forth, and they lived there with their parents for ages before they came here." (*Discourses of*

Brigham Young, sel. John A. Widtsoe [Salt Lake City: Deseret Book Co., 1941], p. 50.)

Even a conservative estimate would indicate that we waited a significant amount of time as "single adults" to come to earth, marry, and begin family life as we now know it. In comparison to this lengthy premortal period when we were single, we are married in this life for only a brief time—at most, fifty to seventy years. But the quality of our marriage and family relations during this mortal probation greatly influences whether these privileges will continue in the hereafter.

In the premortal realm the only familial relationships we experienced were those we had as sons or daughters of God and as brothers or sisters to each other. We have never before had the privilege to be intimately involved with a member of the opposite sex in a marriage relationship with the potential to bear children. However, now we are endowed with privileges, relationships, and powers that will never end if we are faithful to the laws and covenants upon which these stewardships are based.

This doctrine ought to influence in a practical way how we treat each other as family members. For example, how could a person who understands marriage and family in this context be abusive to a spouse or child? How could anyone who understands that this existence may be the only opportunity we will ever have to build an eternal kingdom treat a spouse with anything but love and charity? How could a person with this vision of family life use anger to control, manipulate, or intimidate a member of his own household? The person who forsakes responsibilities or goes astray in such sacred family stewardships jeopardizes the continuation of those stewardships in the eternities.

In order to learn effective ways to be married partners and parents, we must help each other to learn how to carry out these callings. To assume that we know all we need to about marriage and parenting, when we have had no experience in these roles before this life and have relatively little time to experience them here, is to invite an array of possible problems.

As we grow in our understanding of who we are and of the potential blessings that await us, if we do get angry or if in our spiritual immaturity we become upset we will seek forgiveness immediately when we realize how foolish we have been. Surely we will regret our offenses and immediately want to restore our relationships through appropriate humility and repentance. We must have things right with the most important people we know! And how grateful and relieved we should be to know that an atonement has been made that allows us to repent, to change. Anger causes a withdrawal of the Spirit of the Lord; that loss should sensitize us to the need to recover its influence.

An understanding of doctrines relating to premortality and the purpose of life can also motivate us to become more Christlike in our relationships. Thus if another is thoughtless or offensive toward us, a Christlike attitude will cause us to forgive quickly, to be filled with charity, for we will realize that perhaps we sometimes say and do things that unintentionally offend others. How easily we forgive little children or a covenant companion when we realize that their motives are not evil! A man or woman is less likely to take offense at the words or actions of any other family member when he or she appreciates the nature of family relationships as it is revealed in the plan of salvation.

Is this not what the gospel plan requires of us if we are to be followers of Christ? Perhaps we sometimes struggle in these areas because we have not connected gospel doctrines to marriage and family relations. When we are ignorant of these principles, or we do not understand them, the carnal side of our nature prevails. And when our vision is obstructed, we act more like "the natural man" than like Christ. Losing our temper, saying hurtful things, or making critical, judgmental statements make us an enemy to God and his purposes. No wonder the gospel is repentance oriented. It becomes clear why the Lord has us renew covenants with him through the sacrament each week to remind us of our dependence on him. When we do not periodically renew our perspective and repent of our sins, we lose the Spirit of the Lord and become insensitive to others' needs and feelings. Carnal man—unrepentant man—justifies and defends offenses and blames others for failure. Such arrogance, pride, and selfishness prevent us from making needed changes that could put us back on the path to eternal life.

Instead of merely "controlling" anger or "dealing with" negative feelings, then, this orientation does not allow these emotions to be generated in the first place, or, if they do begin to surface, it means that we quickly repent as we feel the Spirit withdraw. We *are* free agents. We *can* choose how we respond. We *can* stop using events as an excuse to vent our personal anger and frustrations upon family members. As pointed out earlier, many of us do seem to have this ability to be patient and generous in the dating years. When a date hits a golf ball badly, we are able to laugh. In comparison, if a family member "misses the ball," too often we become angry. Have you ever been upset, when suddenly you received a phone call and you quickly adopted a pleasant tone of voice? The irony is that we are usually more decent to strangers who have no eternal connection to us than we are to those of our own household! When we deal with customers or close friends, we seem to go out of our way not to offend or take offense, because we know that to act publicly on negative emotions brings undesirable consequences. At those times we can exercise self-control and refuse to allow the actions of others to negatively influence our behavior.

It was this ability to choose responses, in part, that made the Savior perfect. Though he was "in all points tempted like as we are" (Hebrews 4:15), he chose not to respond in ways that hurt others. (This is not to say, of course, that he did not sometimes respond with righteous indignation. For example, the hypocrisy of some made it necessary to confront them, in which case *they* chose to take offense at Jesus' chastisement rather than repent.) It appears that the Savior's understanding of doctrine and of his role in the plan of salvation gave him an eternal perspective and a love for his brothers and sisters that made it possible for him not to sin against people. The Book of Mormon emphasizes that pride and selfishness are often reasons why we take offense or remain unforgiving. These sins come as a result of our losing our eternal perspective and allowing our fallen nature to rule. Sometimes we act as if we *enjoy* being offended in order to have an excuse to launch a counteroffensive. Often we hold grudges against others to justify our own position without considering our rationale. At times it seems as if we prefer being cantankerous to being charitable and kind. When we choose these negative responses, we are behaving more like people who are in a "carnal state," or a "state contrary to the nature of happiness" (Alma 41:11), a situation that undoubtedly delights our enemy Satan.

The Lord said in a modern revelation: "Ye ought to forgive

one another; for he that forgiveth not his brother his trespasses standeth condemned before the Lord; for there remaineth in him the greater sin. I, the Lord, will forgive whom I will forgive, but of you it is required to forgive all men. And ye ought to say in your hearts—let God judge between me and thee, and reward thee according to thy deeds." (D&C 64:9–11.) How could Saints who are sure of the doctrine do otherwise? No wonder repentance is at the heart of the Atonement and is critical to our progress. Repentance allows us to clear any negative behavior with both God and family members.

Even when we have an eternal perspective, understand our premortal heritage, and appreciate the purposes of our lives, these concepts must be reviewed frequently. Without such frequent review, we do not have the ability, with our mortal limitations, to retain in our minds the importance of all the doctrines of the gospel. Thus it becomes paramount that we review gospel principles (now we see the reason for daily scripture study) to keep our perspective and faith strong.

The Degrees of Glory

Scripture from the Doctrine and Covenants clarifies that only those couples who attain the highest degree of glory will remain sealed following the resurrection (see D&C 131:1–4; 132:15–17). Such couples are said to possess the power of "eternal lives" (see D&C 132:20–24). Without a temple marriage, a man and woman cannot come forth in the resurrection and enjoy these blessings. Those who do marry in the temple enter into the same covenant that Abraham made with God, wherein he was promised innumerable seed and the powers of eternal increase (see Abraham 2:9–11; Genesis 13:16; 22:17). Elder Bruce R. McConkie wrote: "Those portions of [the Abrahamic covenant] which pertain to personal exaltation and eternal increase are renewed with each member of the house of Israel who enters the order of celestial marriage" (*Mormon Doctrine,* p. 13).

These blessings are available today because of Elias's return to the Kirtland Temple on 6 April 1836. Elias "committed the dispensation of the gospel of Abraham, saying that in us and our seed all generations after us should be blessed" (D&C 110:12). Such blessings are associated with a temple sealing.

The Damnation and Curse of Lucifer

Satan will never marry or have children, and he wants all of us to be in the same condition. He does not want any who kept their first estate and who now have these blessings in their second estate to retain them in eternity. He knows that if we misuse the powers associated with marriage and the family, we may forfeit the blessings promised to those who gain exaltation; hence his intense efforts to coax us into such misuse. Elder Orson Pratt explained why not only Satan but also those who gain degrees of glory less than the highest will be denied the blessings of exaltation:

> God . . . has ordained that the highest order and class of beings that should exist in the eternal worlds should exist in the capacity of husbands and wives, and that they alone should have the privilege of propagating their species. . . . Now it is wise, no doubt, in the Great Creator to thus limit this great and heavenly principle to those who have arrived or come to the highest state of exaltation, . . . to dwell in His presence, that they by this means shall be prepared to bring up their spirit offspring in all pure and holy principles in the eternal worlds, in order that they may be made happy. Consequently, He does not entrust this privilege of multiplying spirits with the terrestrial or telestial, or the lower order of beings there, nor with angels. But why not? Because they have not proved themselves worthy of this great privilege. (In *Journal of Discourses* 13:186.)

In other words, such individuals suffer "the deaths" (D&C 132:25) in that they do not enjoy the blessings of exaltation and eternal increase. On another occasion Elder Pratt wrote on a similar theme:

> Could wicked and malicious beings, who have eradicated every feeling of love from their bosoms, be permitted to propagate their species, the offspring would partake of all the evil, wicked, and malicious nature of their parents. . . . It is for this

reason that God will not permit the fallen angels to multiply: it is for this reason that God has ordained marriages for the righteous only [in eternity]: it is for this reason that God will put a final stop to the multiplication of the wicked after this life: it is for this reason that none but those who have kept the celestial law will be permitted to multiply after the resurrection. ("Celestial Marriage," *The Seer*, October 1853, p. 157.)

As we reflect on these two statements we can more fully appreciate that we have an important mission to accomplish in this phase of our existence, and that our time on earth to obtain a body, learn self-government, prove ourselves valiant to eternal principles, marry, and rear a posterity is short.

Rearing the Children of Heavenly Father

The Lord places a great trust in us when we become parents, for we bring his children to their mortal life on earth. If all couples decided not to have children (and many in our society are making such a decision), the Father's plan would come to a halt. We are to assist him in his great work. We bring his children to mortality to enjoy the same blessings granted us.

Can you think of a greater trust given two people than to have the Father's children assigned directly to them? Would not heavenly parents have a great interest in how their children were being raised and treated during their mortal life and appreciate the care we give their children? Oh, if only we fully understood this principle of trust in rearing these special spirits!

Doctrine Leads to Christlike Attributes

When a person understands these basic doctrines, he desires to emulate the Savior, the great Exemplar. Becoming as he is means that we develop the same traits and characteristics that he modeled and taught during his earthly ministry. Using the Doctrine and Covenants we can identify many of these traits, which can assist us in our efforts to perfect our family relations. How could marriage fail if each spouse incorporated into his or her nature these attributes?

Christlike Traits

- *Charity* (D&C 4:5–6; 6:19; 12:8; 42:31, 45; 52:40; 59:6; 108:7)
- *Faithfulness* (D&C 5:22; 9:13; 10:69; 50:5)
- *Gentleness* (D&C 121:41)
- *Gratitude* (D&C 59:7, 15)
- *Honesty* (D&C 8:1; 124:15)
- *Hopefulness* (D&C 18:19)
- *Humility* (D&C 1:28; 12:8; 20:37; 29:2; 54:3; 104:79; 112:10)
- *Joyfulness* (D&C 19:39)
- *Meekness* (D&C 19:23; 25:5, 14; 32:1; 38:41)
- *Mercy* (D&C 64:9)
- *Modesty* (D&C 42:40)
- *Patience* (D&C 4:6; 6:19; 24:8; 31:9; 63:66; 67:13; 98:23–24; 107:30; 121:41)
- *Peaceableness* (D&C 98:16)
- *Prayerfulness* (D&C 6:11, 14–15; 9:8; 10:5; 19:38; 30:6; 31:12; 46:7)
- *Purity* (D&C 100:16)
- *Seeking for Wisdom* (D&C 16:7)
- *Temperance* (D&C 4:6; 6:19; 12:8; 107:30)
- *Virtue* (D&C 38:24; 46:33)

My thesis is this: If we were to incorporate these traits into our personalities and characters, our spouses would be thrilled to be our companions and our children would be honored to be our posterity! Think in terms of what the Savior requires of his disciples if they are to qualify for eternal life.

The more we emulate our Exemplar, the more lovable we become. The more we follow the way of the natural man—the way Satan would encourage us to go—the more repulsive we are. Our goal is to be like the Master, who was perfect in every way—emotionally, spiritually, mentally, and physically. When we understand his mission we have a great love for him and an appreciation of the redemption he accomplished for us; and it is our goal then to become as Christ is if we want to build an eternal marriage.

Summary

When we understand the doctrines of the Church more fully and become familiar with their application, we begin to apply these principles to our relationships with others because we understand their impact on our quest for eternal life. Such doctrines empower us to discipline our lives to be the kind of husbands and wives, fathers and mothers who have developed Christlike traits and character attributes so that we can live together in love in this life as a prelude to eternal life in the next.

Upon understanding the doctrines of the Atonement, the premortal life, the degrees of glory, the eternal curse placed on Lucifer and those who follow him, and the origin of our children as the offspring of God, we gain a new appreciation for the purpose of life and how God would have us live and act. As we abide the laws, covenants, and principles of the gospel of Jesus Christ, we prepare ourselves for the blessings of exaltation. The Atonement can compensate for our sins and our errors as we progress toward immortality and eternal life if we repent and allow the Savior's sacrifice to be effective in our lives. With an eternal perspective we truly can fulfill our destiny of immortality and eternal life.

CHAPTER FOUR

Why the Lord Needs Great Families in These Latter Days

We live in the latter days, a period designated by the Lord as the "dispensation of the fulness of times" (D&C 112:30). This means, simply, that *all* doctrines, principles, and priesthood keys and ordinances essential for us to qualify for eternal life have been restored to the earth once again (see D&C 124:41). An important part of this restoration includes the power to organize eternal families through ordinances available in modern temples.

The Lord established marriage as an eternal compact between a man and wife, with the intent that their earthly posterity would be bound to them forever. A temple marriage, or sealing of a man and wife, therefore, is the crowning ordinance of the gospel. Due to the sacred nature of these ordinances, God has commanded us to build temples so that a man and wife can enter into the order of marriage and through their righteousness qualify for exaltation in the highest degree of glory, the only heavenly glory where families reside (see D&C 131:1–2). However, as we shall see, very few of the Father's family who have lived on the earth have had the opportunity to obtain these blessings. The history of the world reveals a series of apostasies necessitating the Lord's removal of the gospel and priesthood from his children because of their wickedness and rejection of eternal principles. When a new generation so merited, he restored the saving principles and ordinances by raising up a new prophet.

Like all good parents, Heavenly Father wants his children to develop their full potential and become as he is. His spirit children have been coming to this earth to work out their salvation for thousands of years, with varying degrees of success. In general, it has not gone well—rarely, it seems, has a people wanted to live so that they might attain the ultimate reward, exaltation.

In order to appreciate the need God has for husbands and wives, mothers and fathers to carry out his purposes in this final dispensation, we must be aware of what has transpired in previous dispensations and thus come to understand where we fit in this final winding-up scene. Former-day prophets have looked down the stream of time to our day, rejoicing in the magnitude and scope of this latter-day period that includes the establishment of Zion on the earth (see D&C 121:26–27). From Adam to the current Church President, every prophet has labored valiantly to bring his people to live the ultimate plan of happiness—the gospel of Jesus Christ. It has been a difficult task.

From the beginning, the Lord has revealed his reasons for creating and peopling the earth. He explained to Moses that his dual purposes are "to bring to pass the immortality and eternal life of man" (Moses 1:39). To date, there have been seven major dispensations of the gospel and priesthood to the earth, beginning with Adam and Eve. Let us look more carefully at each of these dispensations.

Adam and Eve

The fall of Adam and Eve gave our first parents the ability to have children and begin the peopling of this planet with

God's premortal spirit children. These two were commanded to "multiply, and replenish the earth" (Genesis 1:28). They transgressed God's law and were expelled from the Garden of Eden, thereby initiating the great plan of mortality.

As their seed, we find ourselves in a fallen condition, in need of a Savior and the principles of redemption. Jesus Christ was foreordained to be that Savior from the foundation of the world, the one who would overcome the effects of the drastic change that brought mortality. Unfortunately, many of the descendants of Adam and Eve refused to accept the gospel. Those who were righteous became heirs of gospel and priesthood blessings that enabled righteous men and women, by obedience to heavenly laws and the atonement of Christ, to overcome their fallen condition and return to the Father's presence.

Adam and Eve did not evolve, nor were they prehistoric creatures or cavemen—they were children of God (see Moses 6:22). We learn that Adam and Eve were intelligent beings, capable of reading and writing in a pure (Adamic) language. "And a book of remembrance was kept," the record says, "in the which was recorded, in the language of Adam, for it was given unto as many as called upon God to write by the spirit of inspiration; and by them their children were taught to read and write, having a language which was pure and undefiled" (Moses 6:5–6).

Adam, one of the great spirits in the premortal life, helped create the earth. He was known then as Michael (see D&C 107:54). Near the end of his long and productive life, Adam gathered all of his righteous posterity together at Adam-ondi-Ahman. The Lord appeared at this gathering and administered comfort to Adam and acknowledged his faithfulness (see D&C 107:53–57). Adam prophesied concerning his posterity "unto the latest generation" of time (see D&C 107:56). Through the corridor of time he saw the glories and tragedies, the successes and failures that would come to his children as world events unfolded, even down to our own day and beyond. He died at the age of 930.

After the tragedy of Cain's murder of Abel, Adam and Eve were blessed with another son, Seth. Scripture records a priesthood blessing given to him by his father, Adam: "This order [of priesthood] was instituted in the days of Adam, and came down by lineage in the following manner: from Adam to Seth, who was ordained by Adam at the age of sixty-nine years, and was blessed by him three years previous to his (Adam's) death, and received the promise of God by his father, that his posterity should be the chosen of the Lord, and that they should be preserved unto the end of the earth" (D&C 107:41–42).

Seth's blessing contained two important elements: (1) his children were to be the chosen of the Lord, and (2) his descendants were to always be found on the earth.

The first concept, that of being chosen, is often misunderstood to imply some type of spiritual superiority. Actually, it has to do with service. A person is chosen because he possesses the gospel and priesthood and is called to minister to those who are less active or who are unaware that such blessings exist. The chosen—faithful members of the Church—are obligated to share gospel principles and to administer priesthood ordinances to those who have not yet obtained them (see D&C 88:80–82).

The second part of Seth's blessing, that he would always have a descendant living on the earth, means that even in these latter days there must be literal progeny of Seth in the flesh. Who are these individuals? Could you be one of them? Would you want to be?

As a matter of fact, when you received a patriarchal blessing, you learned that you are of Israel, whose lineage traces back to Seth. The Lord's promises to Seth are still in process of fulfillment. Though men and women may be spiritually inconsistent in the way they live the gospel, the Lord always keeps his part of the covenant. Blessings are often delayed, but covenants will be fulfilled if and when individuals and nations qualify.

Enoch

A faithful descendant in the patriarchal chain was Enoch. The people from the time of Adam to Enoch, a period of about seven hundred years, were generally wicked. Enoch was called to reclaim them:

> And he heard a voice from heaven, saying: Enoch, my son, prophesy unto this people, and say unto them—Repent, for thus

saith the Lord: I am angry with this people, and my fierce anger is kindled against them; for their hearts have waxed hard, and their ears are dull of hearing, and their eyes cannot see afar off;

And for these many generations, ever since the day that I created them, have they gone astray, and have denied me, and have sought their own counsels in the dark; and in their own abominations have they devised murder, and have not kept the commandments, which I gave unto their father, Adam (Moses 6:27–28).

Enoch began his ministry among a wicked people. He labored diligently to change their hearts. After some success, sufficient conflict arose between Enoch's people and the unbelievers that the latter tried to destroy the former. The Lord fought in behalf of Enoch and his people.

And so great was the faith of Enoch that he led the people of God, and their enemies came to battle against them; and he spake the word of the Lord, and the earth trembled, and the mountains fled, even according to his command; and the rivers of water were turned out of their course; and the roar of the lions was heard out of the wilderness; and all nations feared greatly, so powerful was the word of Enoch, and so great was the power of the language which God had given him (Moses 7:13).

Enoch's people prevailed, and during a period of 365 years, while evil was widespread outside their community, Enoch lifted his people to such a level of righteousness that "the Lord came and dwelt with" them (Moses 7:16). As individuals become sanctified they gather with others of a similar nature and disposition; collectively they are called Zion. They establish a place where the pure in heart can live, work, and worship together. In reality, that is the goal of every prophet—to sanctify a people so that the powers of heaven can be manifested to the degree that even God himself can come and dwell among them.

Eventually Enoch and his city, Zion, were translated, being "taken up into heaven" (Moses 7:21; see also v. 69). "And [Enoch] saw the Lord," latter-day scripture tells us, "and he walked with him, and was before his face continually; and he walked with God three hundred and sixty-five years, making him four hundred and thirty years old when he was translated" (D&C 107:49). Elder Bruce R. McConkie stated: "The holy priesthood did more to perfect men in the days of Enoch than at any other time. Known then as the order of Enoch (see D&C 76:57), it was the power by which he and his people were translated. And they were translated because they had faith and exercised the power of the priesthood." ("The Doctrine of the Priesthood," *Ensign,* May 1982, p. 32.)

As Latter-day Saints, we have the same goal, to build a people who will become pure in heart in anticipation of the Lord's second coming. After that event, Enoch and his city will return to the earth. (See Moses 7:62–63.) Enoch's dispensation is one of the bright spots in the history of God's dealings with his children.

Noah

The translation of Enoch and the righteous from the earth left Noah with an unenviable task—to work with those who literally could not get off the ground! After the time of Enoch, righteous individuals (except for those who had missions to fulfill on earth) were translated to Enoch's city (see Moses 7:27). During the latter stages of Noah's mission, however—that is, during the one hundred twenty years prior to the Flood—apparently there were no converts.

The Lord brought Noah's prophecy of a great flood as a judgment against the wicked, with only Noah, his wife, and his three sons and their companions surviving the great deluge. What a sad climax to Noah's valiant ministry among a people who chose not to be like the people of Enoch! (See Moses 8: 17–30.)

The connection between Noah's day and our own is highlighted in a prophecy of the Lord in which he refers to his second coming: "But as it was in the days of Noah, so it shall be also at the coming of the Son of Man" (Joseph Smith—Matthew 1:41). What was so terrible about Noah's day that has a parallel in our day? The book of Moses describes the conditions in Noah's day this way: "And God saw that the wickedness of men had become great in the earth; and every man was lifted up in the imagination of the thoughts of his heart, being only evil continually" (Moses 8:22).

It is difficult to imagine a society so wicked that "every man" was "evil continually." Because the Savior foresaw similar conditions in our day, we should be alert to any elements in our environment that have the power to corrupt us and contribute to our generation's becoming like the people of Noah's day. May I suggest one threat—namely, the media. In Noah's time the people did not have cable TV, Hollywood script writers, romance novels, pulp magazines, or beer commercials. Today we can bring a tremendous volume of filth right into our living rooms through the medium of television. Latter-day prophets have warned us of the damage that media offerings can do to our morals and have charged fathers to be "watchmen on the tower" concerning what can so easily enter our homes. While it is true that television and the other media can and do provide wholesome enrichment for our lives, it is not difficult to see that the power of TV and other such marvelous inventions has the capacity to contribute to conditions in which "every man" could be "evil continually."

As we observe events and attitudes that indicate that the Savior's prediction is coming to pass, we need spouses and parents who have the courage to monitor and counter the audio and visual poisons of our day that are capable of destroying minds and lives.

Abraham

Following the catastrophic flood, Abraham became the next "restorer" or dispensation head. He was one of the great prophet-leaders of all time because of his obedience to and faith in God. He was honored to be known as the father of the faithful, the father of all those who embrace the gospel from the Flood to the end of the world (see Abraham 2:10).

Abraham came from a background of apostasy and evil in his own family, yet he had a great desire to follow God. "In the land of the Chaldeans, at the residence of my father, I, Abraham saw that it was needful for me to obtain another place of residence and, finding there was greater happiness and peace and rest for me, I sought for the blessings of the fathers, and the right whereunto I should be ordained to administer the same" (Abraham 1:1–2).

Abraham's father, Terah, had apostatized from the truth and was deeply involved in idolatrous practices. In time, wicked priests maneuvered to kill Abraham by sacrificing him to their false gods. Through his faith, prayers, and undoubtedly his foreordination, his life was spared when an angel interceded. He left the land of his birth to find another land where he could minister in righteousness.

Abraham recorded his desires:

> Having been myself a follower of righteousness, desiring also to be one who possessed great knowledge, and to be a greater follower of righteousness, and to possess a greater knowledge, and to be a father of many nations, a prince of peace, and desiring to receive instructions, and to keep the commandments of God, I became a rightful heir, a High Priest, holding the right belonging to the fathers (Abraham 1:2).

Abraham referred to himself as a "rightful heir." An heir is one who inherits or receives something of value from progenitors. What would be so valuable to Abraham that he would not be satisfied until he had obtained it? "It [the priesthood] was conferred upon me from the fathers; it came down from the fathers, from the beginning of time, yea, even from the beginning, or before the foundation of the earth, down to the present time, even the right of the firstborn, or the first man, who is Adam, or first father, through the fathers unto me" (Abraham 1:3).

Abraham sought the same blessings promised the earlier patriarchs. "I sought for mine appointment unto the Priesthood according to the appointment of God unto the fathers concerning the seed" (Abraham 1:4). Now Abraham's intentions were clear! He learned that he was of a lineage that was eligible for the fulness of gospel and all priesthood blessings (see Abraham 1:31). The Lord covenanted with him:

> My name is Jehovah, and I know the end from the beginning; therefore my hand shall be over thee.
>
> And I will make of thee a great nation, and I will bless thee above measure, and make thy name great among all nations, and thou shalt be a blessing unto thy seed after thee, that in their hands they shall bear this ministry and Priesthood unto all nations. (Abraham 2:8–9; see also vv. 10–11.)

Abraham obtained the fulness of the gospel and the priesthood (see D&C 84:14–15). His forefather, Seth, had been
promised that his children would be the chosen of the Lord
(see D&C 107:42), and through Abraham that promise was
continued. Abraham's posterity were also heirs to the gospel
and priesthood, with the obligation and privilege to extend
these blessings to all mankind from that time forth.

The significance of Abraham's blessing in our day is evident
in many ways. For example, in 1974 (and again in 1984),
President Spencer W. Kimball said that all of the young men of
missionary age in the Church should serve the Lord as full-time
proselyters (see *Ensign,* October 1974, pp. 2–14, and *Ensign,*
April 1984, pp. 3–6). In effect, the Lord was renewing the
promises made to Abraham that his seed had the right and
obligation to administer the gospel and priesthood to God's
children throughout the earth. Are there any young men or
women in the Church today who would not be of Abraham's
seed? No. Anyone baptized into the Church becomes the seed
of Abraham. The Lord said:

> And I will bless them through thy name; for as many as re-
> ceive this Gospel shall be called after thy name, and shall be ac-
> counted thy seed, and shall rise up and bless thee, as their father;
> And I will bless them that bless thee, and curse them that
> curse thee; and in thee (that is, in thy Priesthood) and in thy seed
> (that is, thy Priesthood), for I give unto thee a promise that this
> right [to have the gospel and priesthood] shall continue in thee,
> and in thy seed after thee (that is to say, the literal seed, or the
> seed of the body) shall all the families of the earth be blessed,
> even with the blessings of the Gospel, which are the blessings of
> salvation, even of life eternal (Abraham 2:10–11).

What an honor to be of Abraham's seed in these last days!
And what a mission we have before us! A patriarchal blessing
declares lineage for individual Latter-day Saints, and like
Abraham, we must then seek the same blessings of our forbear,
including—

1. Posterity "as innumerable as the stars; or, if ye were to
   count the sand upon the seashore ye could not number
   them" (D&C 132:30). This promise begins in mortality

and continues in the resurrection for those who gain eternal lives.

2. A right to the fulness of the gospel and the priesthood.
3. The calling to take the gospel and priesthood to "all nations" (Abraham 2:9–11).

Blessings of the Abrahamic covenant are sealed upon a couple in a temple marriage, and their ultimate fulfillment is based on the couple's righteousness. Elias restored blessings pertaining to "the dispensation of the gospel of Abraham" in our day to Joseph Smith in the Kirtland Temple in 1836 (see D&C 110:12). The children of couples married in the temple are "born in the covenant," meaning they are heirs to a fulness of the gospel and the priesthood if they live worthily and faithfully claim them through righteousness as did Abraham, their progenitor. The covenant that God made with Abraham extends naturally to his seed; therefore, as his children, we are *eligible* for all that father Abraham possessed, enabling us to qualify for eternal life. Marriage in the temple is mandatory for those who desire to obtain these blessings (see D&C 131:1–4).

In effect, when a husband and wife marry in the temple, each child born to them has the right to serve a mission, the right to the blessings of the priesthood, and a right to the fulness of the gospel—hence to qualify for eternal life. With those rights also comes the obligation to fully exercise them. These blessings of Abraham belong to his lineage and, in our day, to all those who join the Church. Baptism puts one on the path to all the blessings of Abraham. Each person has the responsibility to continue in righteousness until every priesthood ordinance for which he or she is eligible is claimed. Women are eligible to serve missions too, but they are not under the same obligation as those who hold the priesthood.

Faithful young men and women of the Church—as Abraham's seed and as sons and daughters of God who no doubt were valiant in the premortal life—have been reserved to come forth in these latter days. Heavenly Father needs them at this time to help reclaim his children, many of whom "are only kept from the truth because they know not where to find it" (D&C 123:12). God's children are in need of the gospel and the priesthood keys if they are to qualify for exaltation. Properly prepared missionaries are needed desperately, now that countries formerly closed to missionary work are open. It is the right and obligation of these sons and daughters of Seth and Abraham to serve their brothers and sisters as emissaries of God.

These blessings of Abraham are sealed upon a couple when they marry in the temple. Elijah restored the keys to seal them forever if they faithfully live their covenants. President Joseph Fielding Smith explained:

> If we want to receive the fulness of the priesthood of God, then we must receive the fulness of the ordinances of the house of the Lord and keep his commandments. . . .
>
> Let me put this in a little different way. I do not care what office you hold in this Church . . . you cannot receive the fulness of the priesthood unless you go into the temple of the Lord and receive these ordinances of which the Prophet [Joseph] speaks. No man can get the fulness of the priesthood outside of the temple of the Lord. . . .
>
> . . . I want to make this emphatic.
>
> There is no exaltation in the kingdom of God without the fulness of priesthood. (*Doctrines of Salvation,* comp. Bruce R. McConkie, 3 vols. [Salt Lake City: Bookcraft, 1954–56], 3:131–32.)

President Spencer W. Kimball explained the importance of our following Abraham's example of faith and obedience so that we can receive the same reward that Abraham has. "I testify to you," wrote President Kimball, "that we can become as Abraham, who now, as a result of his valiance, 'hath entered into his exaltation and sitteth upon his throne.' (D&C 132:29.)" ("The Example of Abraham," *Ensign,* June 1975, p. 6.) Not only Abraham but also his son Isaac and grandson Jacob have attained a similar state: "Because [Isaac and Jacob] did none other things than that which they were commanded, they have entered into their exaltation, according to the promises, and sit upon thrones, and are not angels but are gods" (D&C 132:37). Now, if Abraham and his immediate descendants have already attained that goal, can we not also achieve the same end if we are faithful and obtain the same principles, ordinances, and blessings?

As Abraham's posterity in the latter days, we too can gain

exaltation if we are faithful in obtaining Abraham's blessings and living worthy of them. Elder Bruce R. McConkie wrote concerning the importance of our seeking these blessings in temples: "The most important things that any member of The Church of Jesus Christ of Latter-day Saints ever does in this world are: 1. To marry the right person, in the right place, by the right authority; and 2. To keep the covenant made in connection with this holy and perfect order of matrimony—thus assuring the obedient persons of an inheritance of exaltation in the celestial kingdom" (*Mormon Doctrine*, 2d ed. [Salt Lake City: Bookcraft, 1966], p. 118).

There are millions of individuals who have lived since the days of Adam for whom ordinance work must yet be done. Teaching them the gospel in the spirit world is the task of righteous Saints who are presently among them (see D&C 138:30, 57). But there is no need for us to wait for the Millennium to assist departed family members. All of the priesthood keys to do work for them are presently on the earth. No wonder President Kimball said: "I feel the same sense of urgency about temple work for the dead as I do about the missionary work for the living, since they are basically one and the same" ("The True Way of Life and Salvation," *Ensign*, May 1978, p. 4).

Moses

The blessings conferred upon Abraham were intended to continue through Isaac, Jacob, Joseph, and their posterity forever. But a serious problem developed between the time of Joseph and Moses. The entire family of Israel was taken captive in Egypt and became slaves! They were in bondage for generations. How could such a thing happen to a people who were chosen to be the missionary force to save the world?

We learn an important lesson from this experience: A testimony of the gospel is not passed through the chromosomes and genes! Salvation is not a right, nor is it granted simply because one's parents marry in the temple or because one is an heir to certain blessings through lineage. Only consistent and faithful observance of the commandments and living the principles of the gospel will do it. One may be an heir to eternal life through lineage, but only righteousness ensures that such promises will be realized. (See Romans 9:6; 2 Nephi 30:2.)

The Lord raised up Moses to reclaim His people, who were mired in apostasy and bondage, and to restore to them the same blessings given Abraham. Moses' challenge was to prepare a people to come into God's presence, as modern scripture informs us:

> And this greater priesthood administereth the gospel and holdeth the key of the mysteries of the kingdom, even the key of the knowledge of God.
>
> Therefore, in the ordinances thereof, the power of godliness is manifest.
>
> And without the ordinances thereof, and the authority of the priesthood, the power of godliness is not manifest unto men in the flesh;
>
> For without this no man can see the face of God, even the Father, and live.
>
> Now this Moses plainly taught to the children of Israel in the wilderness, and sought diligently to sanctify his people that they might behold the face of God;
>
> But they hardened their hearts and could not endure his presence; therefore, the Lord in his wrath, for his anger was kindled against them, swore that they should not enter into his rest while in the wilderness, which rest is the fulness of his glory.
>
> Therefore, he took Moses out of their midst, and the Holy Priesthood also:
>
> And the lesser priesthood continued. (D&C 84:19–26.)

What a tragedy! Without the Melchizedek Priesthood, the children of Israel lost their right to the fulness of gospel and priesthood blessings, with only the prophets retaining these powers. Even the individual right to the Holy Ghost was taken away. A prolonged night of darkness ensued from the time of Moses down to Jesus Christ, approximately fifteen hundred years. A chosen people were denied blessings to which they were entitled by lineage but which they forfeited through transgression. A proud people stumbled. Most of these Israelites were scattered with the lost tribes. The Jews were later taken captive after Lehi departed Jerusalem and were carried to Babylon. What a sad culmination to the efforts of Moses, Joshua, David, and Solomon to restore them to their rightful blessings as descendants of Jacob!

Jesus Christ

Jesus came as a restorer and as the Redeemer. Before his day, a remnant of Jews had returned from the Babylonian captivity and settled in the area of Jerusalem. They rebuilt the temple of Solomon and laid claim to Abraham's lineage and blessings. But both John the Baptist and Jesus chastised them for their hypocritical and corrupted lifestyles, even though their lineage was through the great patriarchs Abraham and Judah. The Savior challenged their claims to spiritual superiority based on genealogy (see John 8:33–40).

Jacob, Nephi's brother, described the extent of the people's wickedness: "It must needs be expedient that Christ . . . should come among the Jews, among those who are the more wicked part of the world; and they shall crucify him—for thus it behooveth our God, and there is none other nation on earth that would crucify their God. . . . But because of priestcrafts and iniquities, they at Jerusalem will stiffen their necks against him, that he be crucified." (2 Nephi 10:3, 5.)

The Apostles carried the work of the Lord to other nations but were unsuccessful in establishing much of a permanent base. Apostasy from within and influences from without caused the Church to be driven into the wilderness (see Revelation 12:6).

Joseph Smith

Even though the Savior restored the fulness of the gospel and priesthood in his day, it remained on the earth through his Apostles for only a brief period. Following Jesus' death and that of the Twelve, another long night of apostasy settled upon the world until the Restoration through the Prophet Joseph Smith. Through angelic ministers the Lord brought again to the earth sufficient gospel principles and priesthood power to enable his children to qualify for eternal life.

What a privilege to be born in the latter days and to have the opportunity to embrace the gospel and obtain the essential ordinances of exaltation! As Latter-day Saints we have a special opportunity to do what has rarely been accomplished since Enoch's day—establish a Zion people who are worthy and prepared for the Savior's presence. We must not be sidetracked. There is much at stake; so many of our faithful progenitors from earlier dispensations are dependent on our progress as a people and as a church to do family history research and perform temple ordinances in their behalf.

It is our privilege to take the gospel to the entire world so that a people might be sanctified and prepared when the Lord comes again to the earth to dwell among his Saints and inaugurate the great work of the Millennium. Thus the overall mission of the Church is to "invite all to come unto Christ" (D&C 20:59) "and be perfected in him" (Moroni 10:32), and this mission has three aspects as follows:

1. Proclaim the gospel to every nation, kindred, tongue, and people. Every able and worthy young man and many sisters and married couples are needed to serve full-time missions. Every member, too, should share the gospel.
2. Perfect the Saints by preparing them to receive gospel ordinances and by caring for those in need. Through service, personal righteousness, and bringing back to the fold those who have lost their way, we can help bring about Zion.
3. Redeem the dead by performing vicarious gospel ordinances for them.

If we are to succeed in these profound tasks, our homes will need to be the center of influence for children who understand the need the Lord has for them to serve missions. Too, we have Church members in need of reactivation. Home and visiting teaching and other Church programs can help in reclaiming these individuals. Clearly millions have lived and died without access to the required ordinances and teachings of the gospel.[1] Thus our task is to complete as much genealogical and temple work as we can before the return of the Lord.

---

1. It has been estimated that at least sixty to seventy billion people have lived on the earth since Adam and Eve. Given such numbers, it is obvious to see that we must continue to build more temples, activate members to temple work, and increase our research. However, during the Millennium only work for those who have accepted the gospel in the spirit world will be done; presently we do ordinance work for all those we identify, without knowing their worthiness or acceptance (see Joseph Fielding Smith, *Doctrines of Salvation* 2:176).

Here's the catch! The only people who can actually perform ordinances in behalf of the dead are mortal beings—flesh and blood bodies. Resurrected, translated, or spirit beings do not do their own ordinance work. "Will resurrected beings during the millennium actually take part in the endowment work of the temple along with mortal beings?" President Joseph Fielding Smith asked rhetorically. "The answer to this question is no! That is, they will not assist in performing the ordinances. Resurrected beings will assist in furnishing information which is not otherwise available, but mortals will have to do the ordinance work in the temples." (*Doctrines of Salvation* 2:178.) Mortal people must perform vicarious work for those in the spirit world. That means that when the Savior comes there must be a sanctified people living in the flesh who will complete this work. Our task is to be worthy and willing to make up for thousands of years of apostasy when people were lost and scattered. Thus the need for another Zion similar to that of Enoch.

We need to ask ourselves, How are we doing as a church and a people? How is our dispensation progressing? We have completed well over 160 years since the Restoration was inaugurated. Are we more like Enoch's people, or do we resemble those of Moses? Is building Zion an important goal or simply something nice to sing about in our hymns? Do we understand our mission and what we must accomplish? The leaders of earlier dispensations are now looking to us to fulfill the Lord's purposes in this final dispensation. We read in the Doctrine and Covenants: "God shall give unto you [Saints of the latter days] knowledge by his Holy Spirit, yea, by the unspeakable gift of the Holy Ghost, that has not been revealed since the world was until now; which our forefathers have awaited with anxious expectation to be revealed in the last times, which their minds were pointed to by the angels" (D&C 121:26–27).

Do you think that these forefathers—Adam, Noah, Abraham, Moses, the Apostles, and the Nephite faithful—are anxious about our accomplishing our latter-day mission? (See D&C 128:18–21.) Is our success automatic? No, we must work diligently to bring about the fulfillment of the promises the Lord made with them in earlier days. Great blessings await those who labor unceasingly to move the latter-day work along. Nephi recorded these words of the Lord: "And blessed are they who shall seek to bring forth my Zion at that day [our day], for they shall have the gift and the power of the Holy Ghost; and if they endure unto the end they shall be lifted up at the last day, and shall be saved in the everlasting kingdom of the Lamb; and whoso shall publish peace, yea, tidings of great joy, how beautiful upon the mountains shall they be" (1 Nephi 13:37).

Our success will be assured if righteous mothers and fathers conscientiously teach their children of their heritage and foreordination, testify to them regarding the mission of the Church in these latter days, and set a righteous example. The quality of family life is the key to our success in inviting all to truly come unto Christ.

Israel, are we ready? Can we make a Zion society flourish once again on the earth? Can we do it in a world similar to that of Noah? In the midst of prosperity? We too are heirs to the blessings of Abraham. Will we muster the courage to set our own style of living? Can we survive the temptations of Satan that would delay us or distract us from our goals? Do we have the faith and commitment to move the Lord's kingdom forward? Do we care enough about other brothers and sisters who are unaware of these doctrines to share our blessings and gifts with them, and to activate those presently lost to the work? Can we sanctify our membership, work on family history, attend to vicarious temple service, and open the door to exaltation for our progenitors?

Our youth can grow up inspired by their patriarchal blessings and their foreordinations regardless of the efforts of the adversary to destroy this work, if we do our part. Latter-day Saint parents would do well to contemplate this statement from the First Presidency's message in a family home evening manual, published in 1974: "We assure you that you will always have our blessings and our prayers to the end that you may be rewarded by a fulfillment of the promise that if fathers and mothers will discharge this responsibility [of holding family home evenings] not one in a hundred of your family, as has been said by the leaders who have preceded us, would ever go astray" (*Love Makes Our House a Home* [family home evening manual, 1974], p. 2).

It is clear why the prophets have been so adamant in counseling us to make our marriages strong and to carry out the sacred task of parenthood. The spirits sent to us by the Lord are among the most valiant. All essential priesthood keys and powers in conjunction with the fulness of the gospel have been restored.

Summary

Throughout the ages, gospel dispensations have occurred to give God's children the opportunity to prepare for eternal glory. The response has often been disappointing, however. We now live at a time when *all* the blessings of the gospel and priesthood are on the earth. We can compensate, to some extent, for past failures of the house of Israel to respond to their opportunities. If we sense this obligation and understand what God would have us do, perhaps we can avoid the spiritual tragedies of the past. If we achieve Zion again, it will come because our homes are bastions of spiritual strength where the gospel is taught and "caught" by the rising generation. Strong marriages with a clear vision of the future can influence children to adopt gospel values even in an age of general wickedness. We *can* accomplish the great task the Lord has set before us in this final dispensation, and our homes are the place where it must begin. Our forefathers are counting on us.

CHAPTER FIVE

Not Without Hope: Singles and Those "Unequally Yoked"

When you belong to a church that stresses marriage and family life as a requirement for exaltation, and yet as an adult you have never been married, or you are divorced, or maybe your spouse died before you could be sealed in a temple ceremony, there are going to be some questions about your ultimate destiny. Or, if you are married now to a person who isn't interested, so far at least, in qualifying for eternal life, surely there are questions in your mind as to your chances for exaltation in the long run. I think it's important for Church members to understand how the plan of salvation accounts for and covers those who are single, or those who are limited in their progress because of a spouse's disinterest or Church inactivity. Let me share an experience with you to illustrate this point.

After a class one day, a woman (whom I will call Carol) approached me and said, "Brother Brinley, could I visit with you sometime? I *really* need to talk to you." Her eyes and her voice told me that it needed to be now, so I invited her to come to my office for a visit.

After some brief small talk, I asked her how I might help.

She paused, seemed to gather her emotions, and began: "I want you to know that I love my Heavenly Father. I have grown up in the Church. I have a strong testimony of the Restoration. But I need to know, what will happen to me if I don't marry in this life? As *I* understand it, I cannot gain exaltation alone." Then she paused, her eyes dropped, her voice softened almost to a whisper, and she added, "None of my current relationships look too promising."

Now, here was an attractive, articulate single woman, just shy of thirty-four, who wanted so much to marry and be a wife, one who could be a blessing to her husband; and she had a great desire to be a mother. Yet, here she was, unmarried and feeling discouraged; it really hurt her to be alone. I sensed her frustration and asked her to tell me a little about her background.

She began with her high school years, during which she had dated to some extent. "I even went to the junior prom and the senior cotillion," she told me. After graduation from a small high school, she went to a business school for a couple of years of secretarial training, during which time she had what she described as a couple of "close male friends," but nothing serious developed with either one of them. She then found employment as a legal secretary. She dated on occasion but never had what she described as a "firm offer" to marry; in fact, she didn't have any overpowering feeling about any particular person she dated. But as with many others in the Church, her assumption was that if you are active and faithful, marriage will somehow someday happen.

After working for a number of years, she decided to go back to school—the outward reason being to brush up on her computer skills, the inward reason being that she was "just tired of being alone." So far her efforts to find a companion had not been successful. And, like many singles in the Church, she was spiritually down, and wrongly concluded that without marriage the gate to exaltation, at least for her, was forever barred.

There are many singles in the Church, like Carol, who are discouraged with their singleness. Many of these individuals have served missions for the Church. They have a great love for the Lord. They now possess strong testimonies, but they are unsure of their place in the kingdom, and are not clear about how the gospel answers their deep yearnings for the companionship of marriage and the opportunity to be a parent.

Another category of discouraged people are those persons who are married to companions who are not progressing in any Church activity, much less toward a temple sealing. Many of these great souls have tried for years to activate or convert their spouses—without success—and they feel the possibility of an eternal family slipping away as the years go by. Many of these individuals serve faithfully in their callings, and they don't want to settle for less than their full potential. They're concerned about their future here and in the next life as it pertains to marriage and children and exaltation.

Being single beyond a certain age; being alone after a divorce; being a widow or widower whose spouse either was not a member or was not active; being in a discouraging marital situation where a person feels his or her spiritual progress stifled— these are challenges that face a growing number of Church members. And unfortunately our society is not very helpful when it comes to supporting these individuals who want to live the gospel. The media often stereotype divorcées, widows, widowers, singles, or unhappily married couples—often setting them up for exploitation through immoral messages that challenge premarital chastity and marital fidelity. President Ezra Taft Benson stated: "I recognize that most people fall into sexual sin in a misguided attempt to fulfill basic human needs. We all have a need to feel loved and worthwhile. We all seek to have joy and happiness in our lives. Knowing this, Satan often lures people into immorality by playing on their basic needs. He promises leisure, happiness, and fulfillment. But this is, of course, a deception." ("The Law of Chastity," in *Brigham Young University 1987–88 Devotional and Fireside Speeches* [Provo, Utah: University Publications, 1988], p. 50.)

In today's culture, I think it's easy to be misled into thinking that a change from our present situation would resolve all of our problems. And we do live in a day of contrasts, in which there are young and hasty marriages on one hand and long-delayed marriages on the other (people marrying in their thirties, for example). Both early marriages and late marriages may impact negatively on marital stability. Singles usually desire to marry ("If only I were married, I would be happy," one will say), while unhappily married partners wish they were single ("If I could just get out of this marriage, I would be happy," is their tone). Too, we have what are called "no-fault divorces"—with no guarantee that a better marriage will follow. Quick divorces often leave some subsequent singles wondering if they gave up too soon in their marriages. Quite often I will hear one say, "If I had known what it was like to be alone, I think I would have tried harder to make my marriage succeed."

And it seems that we hear more and more about singles experimenting with living with someone, without marriage, trying to find an identity, a missing self, looking for companionship and commitment—by *imitating* marriage. Too, widows and widowers who were never sealed to a companion wonder if they should do proxy work now—when their spouses would not join or be active in the Church in life. Missionary work often brings only one spouse into the Church, which seems to limit the potential of the one who joins.

So these two groups—singles and distressed married persons—ask some penetrating questions: "If marriage is not going to happen to me in this life, will that door be open for me at a later time?" "Is there a way for me to gain exaltation if I married out of the Church?" "Should I divorce my present spouse and try to find one to whom I *can* be sealed?" "What options do I have if *I* am faithful to my own baptism and temple covenants, but my *companion* isn't, when for years I have tried to change his heart—but without success?" "Was my decision to marry out of the Church [usually at an early age] a final decision?" "If marrying out of the faith was a sin, is there a way to repent?" "Is that decision irreversible?" "Is there a way back from this decision I made when I was young and immature?" "I do not want to divorce my spouse, but if she will not come into the Church, should I seek a divorce?" "What will happen to our children?" "My parents were not active and did not have a good marriage, so I never knew what was right and wrong. Their marriage was horrible, and I didn't know any better. Will the Lord consider those factors? Do I still have a chance?"

The questions are many. And the answers are very important. If the plan of salvation can answer these challenges, these people want to know what the answers are. They are anxious to know what relief there is when many of them torture themselves over these issues. And no doubt there are some who have given up, who are defensive about their singleness, who claim they prefer their singleness to marriage. May I repeat a point made earlier in this book, that it is important that we never give up on marriage, for it is the divine plan of our Heavenly Father that we marry if we are to realize our full potential.

Source of Anxiety

Carol and I decided to search out what the Lord has revealed through his latter-day prophets concerning the destiny of singles and of the "unequally yoked."

We decided that much of the concern over marriage stems from this familiar passage from the Doctrine and Covenants: "In the celestial glory there are three heavens or degrees; and in order to obtain the highest, a man must enter into this order of the priesthood [meaning the new and everlasting covenant of marriage]; and if he does not, he cannot obtain it. He may enter into the other, but that is the end of his kingdom; he cannot have an increase." (D&C 131:1–4.) This scriptures leaves little doubt that a temple marriage is a requirement for exaltation.

Before proceeding further, let me be more specific about the categories of people we are talking about. They are as follows:

Singles

1. Men and women faithfully living the gospel who are presently unmarried, divorced, or widowed—that is, without a marriage sealing.[1]
2. Boys and girls who die prior to marriage. They are now living as adult males and females in the spirit world.

---

1. Apparently men have a greater responsibility to pursue marriage than do women. Cultural norms in most countries seem to dictate that men initiate dating and marriage proposals. The counsel is that a man should take the initiative to seek out a companion compatible with his personality and goals. (For example, see Spencer W. Kimball, "The Marriage Decision," *Ensign,* February 1975, pp. 2–6; see also Ezra Taft Benson, "To the Single Adult Brethren of the Church," *Ensign,* May 1988, pp. 51–53.)

3. Individuals, regardless of age, who are mentally or physically incapable of marriage in mortality.

Married Persons

1. A person married outside of the Church. The member is active and would like an eternal family, but his or her spouse refuses to join the Church, making it impossible to organize an eternal family.
2. A Church member married to another member in a civil ceremony. Later, one desires a temple sealing, but the spouse refuses to or cannot qualify.
3. An individual converted to the Church but whose spouse will not join, and the marriage remains intact.
4. A couple who have married in the temple but one of whom fails to live worthy of his or her covenants, preventing an eternal relationship.
5. Couples married in mortal life who lived at a time when the sealing power was not on the earth. Sealing ordinances have not been performed for them, and they are single adults in the spirit world.

As you can see, the fifth category of married persons represents most of the people who have ever lived on the earth, because few people have lived at a time when the fulness of the gospel and priesthood blessings were available. Moreover, a sizeable number of the Church's membership find themselves in one of the above categories. Therefore, it is natural that we would desire answers to these questions concerning those in such situations.

Gospel Perspective

To provide an overall perspective to deal with questions concerning family life and exaltation for singles and those who are unhappily married, let's review several principles.

The Lord explained to Moses that he created innumerable worlds and that His purpose is "to bring to pass the immortality and eternal life" of all God's children (Moses 1:33, 39). Christ administers the gospel under the direction of his Father. The overall plan of salvation is anchored in the Savior's infinite atonement. Now, to be infinite, it must cover every conceivable obstacle we could face in our quest for eternal life. To say it another way, with the wide spectrum of choices we have with our agency, the gospel plan must be broad enough to resolve any universal or personal obstacle that might interfere with our search for eternal life—as long as repentance and change are still possible.

Surely the subject of marriage and family was a major topic of discussion during and after the Council in Heaven, because this is a primary reason we came to the earth (see D&C 49:16–17). Never before, in our long premortal past, were we ever allowed the privilege to marry and have offspring. Can there be any doubt that all kinds of questions about marriage and family would have arisen—such as what happens to individuals born with handicaps who might not marry, or children who die in infancy or childhood, or those who marry but do not like each other, or those who lose a spouse to disease or accident, and so on? These and many other questions must have been discussed and reviewed, and no doubt were answered to our satisfaction. We surely understood the implications and possibilities that could arise in a world of death and physical challenges, and yet we were willing to come to earth knowing that we were taking certain risks in doing so. The point is, the answers must have been fair and reasonable. And certainly we knew the answers to all of these uncertainties at one time, but the veil of forgetfulness drawn across our minds at birth has caused us to forget those answers.

Here we live by faith, and sometimes when the answers are hidden from view or we lack understanding of a principle, our confidence in God and his wisdom is tested. Our mortal minds and hearts are challenged because we cannot see as clearly now as we must have done while in his presence. A review of a few basic elements of the plan of salvation as explained by our latter-day prophets can help both singles and frustrated married partners find satisfaction on this matter.

Each of us was a spirit son or daughter of God before coming to this earth. In 1925, the First Presidency explained that the doctrine of pre-existence "shows that man, as a spirit, was begotten and born of heavenly parents, and reared to maturity in the eternal mansions of the Father, prior to coming upon the earth in a temporal body to undergo an experience in mortality" (in *Messages of the First Presidency,* comp. James R. Clark, 6 vols. [Salt Lake City: Bookcraft, 1965–75], 5:244). In this long pre-mortal setting we learned that to progress we would need to go to a telestial world and obtain a physical body as a counterpart to the spirit body. In this second estate we would be allowed the privilege to marry and create bodies for other spirit brothers and sisters. No doubt we looked forward with great anticipation to this opportunity; for the first time in our personal existence, we would be allowed to marry and become parents. Surely after a long period of time (eons?) in this premortal home, the prospect of moving forward in our quest to be like our heavenly parents was reason enough to shout for joy (see Job 38:7).

Those Who Die Without Hearing the Gospel

Perhaps the best way to understand what future opportunities exist for marriage and family for singles and those un-equally yoked is to understand the familiar principle of what happens to individuals who lived at times when or in places where the gospel and priesthood were not available. In the writings of Paul and Peter (see 1 Corinthians 15:29; 1 Peter 3:18–19; 4:6) and through modern revelation (see D&C 137:7–8; 138), we learn that all of the Father's children will have the opportunity to hear the gospel at some time—if not in this life, then in the spirit world, and certainly before the resurrection and judgment. For these individuals, the essential ordinances of baptism, confirmation, priesthood ordination, endowment, and sealings will be performed in their behalf by temple proxies. The dead are presently learning gospel principles from a missionary force in the spirit world—a topic that is the substance of Doctrine and Covenants 138.

Joseph Smith, in beholding the celestial kingdom in a vision, saw his brother Alvin, and was surprised to learn that Alvin could attain to that degree of glory when he had not been baptized (see D&C 137:5–6). The Lord explained how this was possible: "All who have died without a knowledge of this gospel, who would have received it if they had been permitted to tarry, shall be heirs of the celestial kingdom of God; also all that shall die henceforth without a knowledge of it, who would have received it with all their hearts, shall be heirs of that kingdom; for I, the Lord, will judge all men according to their works, according to the desire of their hearts" (D&C 137:7–9).

Many souls, like Alvin, will be taught and will accept the gospel in the spirit world.

Those Who Die Without Marriage or a Worthy Marriage Partner

It was Joseph Smith who said: "All your losses will be made up to you in the resurrection, provided you continue faithful. By the vision of the Almighty I have seen it." (*Teachings of the Prophet Joseph Smith,* sel. Joseph Fielding Smith [Salt Lake City: Deseret Book Co., 1938], p. 296.) This statement becomes the basic principle behind our coming to terms with some of the apparent inequities of our lives.

Then we have this early statement by President Lorenzo Snow:

A lady came into our office the other day and asked to see me on a private matter. She informed me that she felt very badly, because her opportunities for getting a husband had not been favorable. She was about thirty years of age, and she wanted to know what her condition would be in the other life, if she did not succeed in getting a husband in this life. I suppose this question arises in the hearts of our young people, especially the marriageable sisters and the young widows; and some very foolish doctrine has been presented to some of the sisters in regard to this and other things of a kindred nature. I desire to give a little explanation for the comfort and consolation of parties in this condition. There is no Latter-day Saint who dies after having lived a faithful life who will lose anything because of having failed to do certain things when opportunities were not furnished him or her. In other words, if a young man or a young woman has no opportunity of getting married, and they live faithful lives up to the time of their death, they will have all the blessings, exaltation, and glory that any man or woman will have who had this opportunity and improved it.

That is sure and positive. (*The Teachings of Lorenzo Snow,* comp. Clyde J. Williams [Salt Lake City: Bookcraft, 1984], pp. 137–38.)

Years later, President Harold B. Lee, in a talk given at a Relief Society general conference, used the example of Joseph Smith's brother Alvin to reassure the sisters that the Lord will judge us not only by our actions but also by the intents of our hearts. After quoting what is now Doctrine and Covenants 137:7, President Lee commented: "Thus, wives and mothers who have been denied the blessings of wifehood or motherhood in this life—who say in their heart, if I could have done, I would have done, or I would give if I had, but I cannot for I have not—the Lord will bless you as though you had done, and the world to come will compensate for those who desire in their hearts the righteous things that they were not able to do because of no fault of their own" ("Maintain Your Place as a Woman," *Ensign,* February 1972, p. 56).

President Spencer W. Kimball also taught this principle that persons who, through no fault of theirs, remain unmarried in this life can qualify for the blessings of marriage in the next life. It seems reasonable to assume also that the following words from President Kimball, spoken in the 1978 women's fireside, may also apply to those who are faithful but whose spouse will not qualify for eternal life: "Just as those who do not hear the gospel in this life, but who would have received it with all their hearts had they heard it, will be given the fulness of the gospel blessings in the next world—so, too, the women of the Church who do not in this life have the privileges and blessings of a temple marriage, through no fault of their own, who would have responded if they had an appropriate opportunity—will receive all those blessings in the world to come" ("Privileges and Responsibilities of Sisters," *Ensign,* November 1978, p. 103). The "world to come" I assume to be the spirit world, the next stage of our existence.

In an *Ensign* article, President Kimball explained:

> To you women, we can only say we have no control over the heartbeats or the affections of men, but pray that you may find fulfillment. And in the meantime, we promise you that insofar as eternity is concerned, no soul will be deprived of rich and high

and eternal blessings for anything which that person could not help, that the Lord never fails in his promises, and that every righteous person will receive eventually all to which the person is entitled and which he or she has not forfeited through any fault of his or her own. We encourage both men and women to keep themselves well-groomed, well-dressed, abreast of the times, attractive mentally, spiritually, physically, and especially morally, and then they can lean heavily upon the Lord's promises for these heavenly blessings. ("The Importance of Celestial Marriage," *Ensign*, October 1979, p. 5.)

In the 1979 women's fireside, President Kimball repeated the promise: "Be assured, too, that all faithful sisters, who, through no fault of their own, do not have the privilege during their second estate of being sealed to a worthy man, will have that blessing in eternity. On occasions when you ache for that acceptance and affection which belong to family life on earth, please know that our Father in Heaven is aware of your anguish, and that one day he will bless you beyond your capacity to express." ("The Role of Righteous Women," *Ensign*, November 1979, p. 103.)

In his address given at the 1988 general women's meeting, President Ezra Taft Benson assured faithful but never-married women of eventual blessings of marriage and motherhood: "I also recognize that not all women in the Church will have an opportunity for marriage and motherhood in mortality. But if those of you in this situation are worthy and endure faithfully, you can be assured of all blessings from a kind and loving Heavenly Father—and I emphasize *all blessings*. I assure you that if you have to wait even until the next life to be blessed with a choice companion, God will surely compensate you."

In that same address, President Benson declared: "My humble desire for the wonderful single adult sisters of the Church is that you will receive all that the Father hath, 'even an hundred fold, yea, more.' And I promise you that indeed you will. All of the blessings of our Father in Heaven will be yours if you continue faithful, if you are true, and if you serve Him and His children with all your heart, might, mind, and strength." ("To the Single Adult Sisters of the Church," *Ensign*, November 1988, p. 97.)

President Gordon B. Hinckley addressed the 1991 general women's meeting, saying: "Some who are not married, through no fault of their own, ask whether they will always be denied the highest degree of glory in that kingdom. I am confident that under the plan of a loving Father and a divine Redeemer, no blessing of which you are otherwise worthy will forever be denied you." ("Daughters of God," *Ensign,* November, 1991, p. 98.)

After Carol and I had reviewed these statements together, she commented: "I notice that most of them used the phrase 'through no fault of their own.' What did these General Authorities mean by that?"

"I suppose it means you must never give up hope," I responded, "or become a fatalist or a martyr or say to yourself, 'Well, I'll just wait until the next life, then find a spouse. I'll just stop looking for a companion now, since I'm not having much luck. If no one wants to marry me in this life, I'll let the Lord worry about it later!' If that were your attitude, I think such statements would indicate a lack of faith in God and his plan of salvation—expecting too much of the Lord, with little effort on our part."

"I know," she said. "I have a number of friends who have given up on marriage; they are upset with men, and they are satisfied with being single, and claim they are not even interested in marriage anymore."

"I don't think you can lose faith in marriage, because it is a requirement for the blessings of exaltation.

"Another possibility of fault," I continued, "may be that you can disqualify yourself through repeated sinning. I think that sin closes the door to any future opportunities that could be available to these individuals." I told Carol that some comments by Elder Dean L. Larsen were relevant in this regard:

> We understand that all worthy Saints will eventually have the opportunity to make the covenants of eternal marriage, whether or not that privilege becomes a reality in mortal life. This tenet of our faith should not, however, be understood to mean that those who willfully procrastinate or knowingly avoid the responsibilities of celestial marriage will forever have that opportunity open to them. The Lord will not be mocked in this matter. He sets the requirements and the conditions; we do not. We are free to follow

our own wills in this and other equally important matters, but we are not free to determine the ultimate consequences of these choices. ("Marriage and the Patriarchal Order," *Ensign,* September 1982, p. 6.)

I continued: "Carol, as we read these quotes, it seems to me that you are not to give up hope in this life that you may yet marry. And certainly you must do your part. You can't become careless in your appearance, or let yourself become unattractive; and surely you must remain thoughtful and prayerful about marriage. Then, after all you can do to find a companion, on your own and with the Lord's help, if you are not successful, there is a safety net under you. The opportunity will still be open. The Lord, through his prophets, seems to be assuring you that you will have all the blessings you desire relative to marriage and family life, if you remain faithful.

"Of course, our world here is not perfect, as you know. Cultural norms in our part of the world dictate that men initiate dating. Whether that is right or wrong, I don't know, but clearly men in our culture have an advantage in initiating marriage relationships. However, you will notice that men also seem to be more accountable to the Lord if they fail to actively seek a mate. Now, if no man invites you to join him in marriage, or if the one asking is not your equal in most ways—without your being overly picky, of course—you will have an opportunity to find a companion in the next life, meaning the spirit world."

She wrinkled her brow. "How would that be possible?"

"Well, let's think about this. Suppose, for a moment, that you do not marry in this life."

"Okay, I can handle that," she said. "I seem to be headed that direction anyway."

"All right, then, when you die and enter the spirit world, who else is single there too?"

"I suppose there are many who lived on the earth in earlier times who were single too."

"Men and women?"

"Yes."

"For example, what single men are there?"

"Well, there were many over the centuries who died or were killed without ever marrying, or who lived when the gospel and priesthood were not on the earth—"

I jumped in. "Okay, then you see what I mean."

"Yes, but so what?"

"Well, as these people are taught the principles of the gospel by the missionaries and learn the principles of eternal marriage and family, won't many of them accept these principles and be anxious to participate?"

"Well, I hope so," Carol said.

"And if they are worthy and eligible to do so, but are spirits at the time they learn the doctrine of eternal marriage, how will they find partners who may be available?"

"I guess they will be able to seek a companion among the other singles who are there. I imagine that many others will want to be sealed to the same spouse they were married to in mortality—for time only—when the gospel and priesthood were not on the earth."

"I think so. And some have thought that God would just assign two people to be married. I think people in this situation will have the opportunity to exercise their agency in this most important decision. I don't think God does for us what we can do for ourselves.

"However," I continued, "marriage is an earthly ordinance and can only be performed by mortals in earthly temples. And we have no way of knowing who has accepted the gospel once they leave this life, or what relationships have developed in the spirit world—and we will not know until the Millennium. Thus, at that time, when the veil between the spirit world and this world is lifted, individuals who died without marriage but have longed for that opportunity, who are worthy, and who have found a companion in the spirit world will be anxious to have this new relationship sealed in the temple. Certainly we do not lose emotions and feelings just because we die. It seems to me that the spirit world not only must encompass a wide field of missionary work [see D&C 138:57] but also must be a place for the majority of God's children to find eternal companions."

"What did you mean by 'who may be available'?" Carol asked.

"Well, I suppose that there must be some sort of preliminary judgment or separation of people at the time we die into those who have had an opportunity to accept the gospel and didn't and those who have not yet had that chance. Not everyone will be worthy or qualified to marry. It would be useless, don't you think, for individuals destined for the telestial or terrestrial kingdom to still be eligible to find an eternal companion when there will be no marriage in those kingdoms. They remain separate and single forever (see D&C 132:17). But if you are a candidate for eternal life, as Joseph's brother Alvin was at his death, then you will meet others who are also available and eligible and who are interested in finding an eternal companion. In other words, I don't think the Lord would allow you to develop a relationship in the spirit world with someone who could not qualify for marriage beyond this life."

President Joseph Fielding Smith made this comment: "We have people coming to us all the time just as fearful as they can be that a child of theirs who has died will lose the blessings of the kingdom of God unless that child is sealed to someone who is dead. They do not know the wishes of their child who died too young to think of marriage, but they want to go straight to the temple and have a sealing performed. Such a thing as this is unnecessary and in my judgment wrong."

President Smith then explained how the process will work: "The Lord has said through his servants that during the millennium those who have passed beyond and have attained the resurrection will reveal in person to those who are still in mortality all the information which is required to complete the work of these who have passed from this life. Then the dead will have the privilege of making known the things they desire and are entitled to receive. In this way no soul will be neglected and the work of the Lord will be perfected." (*Doctrines of Salvation*, comp. Bruce R. McConkie, 3 vols. [Salt Lake City: Bookcraft, 1954–56], 3:65.)

In his October 1993 general conference address, Elder Dallin H. Oaks expressed this same idea of marriage opportunities and the importance of the Millennium:

> Some who are listening to this message are probably saying, "But what about me?" We know that many worthy and wonderful Latter-day Saints currently lack the ideal opportunities and essential requirements for their progress. Singleness, childlessness, death, and divorce frustrate ideals and postpone the fulfillment of promised blessings. . . . The Lord has promised that in the

eternities no blessing will be denied his sons and daughters who keep the commandments, are true to their covenants, and desire what is right.

Now, notice this statement:

> Many of the most important deprivations of mortality will be set right in the Millennium, which is the time for fulfilling all that is incomplete in the great plan of happiness for all of our Father's worthy children. We know that will be true of temple ordinances. I believe it will also be true of family relationships and experiences. (" 'The Great Plan of Happiness,' " *Ensign,* November 1993, p. 75.)

An earlier member of the Twelve, Elder Melvin J. Ballard, shared his own experience on this matter:

> You mothers worry about your little children [who have died]. We do not perform sealings for them. I lost a son six years of age, and I saw him a man in the spirit world after his death, and I saw how he had exercised his own freedom of choice and would obtain of his own will and volition a companionship, and in due time to him and to all those who are worthy of it shall come all of the blessings and sealing privileges of the house of the Lord. Do not worry over it. They are safe; they are all right.
> Now, then, what of your daughters who have died and have not been sealed to some man? . . . The sealing power shall be forever and ever with this Church, and provisions will be made for them. We cannot run faster than the Lord has provided the way. Their blessings and privileges will come to them in due time. In the meantime, they are safe. (*Melvin J. Ballard: Crusader for Righteousness* [Salt Lake City: Bookcraft, 1966], p. 228.)

"Carol, it appears from the comments of these Church leaders that temple work for faithful people who died without a fulness of gospel and priesthood blessings will be performed in their behalf during the Millennium. The exciting message is that death cannot rob us of any blessing if we are faithful, and I think this includes those who are faithful but whose spouses will not accept or live the fulness of the gospel along with them." I told Carol that Elder Boyd K. Packer summed it up in a conference talk this way: "Any souls who by nature or circumstance are not afforded the blessing of marriage and parenthood, or who innocently must act alone in rearing children and working to support them, will not be denied in the eternities any blessing—provided they keep the commandments. As President Lorenzo Snow promised: 'That is sure and positive.'" (In Conference Report, October 1993, p. 30.)

"That makes me feel a whole lot better," Carol said, somewhat relieved. "But it seems so long until the Millennium."

"I'm sure it does, but you have to have some time to meet and build a relationship with someone, somewhere, before you marry him. Besides, stop looking so far ahead. You have too much to live for in this life, and it's not too late for you. You're only thirty-four. But now, at least, we know that should you die before you marry, that door is not closed to you forever. Besides"—I tried to be a little humorous—"we are getting closer to the Millennium all the time, and an opportunity to be sealed to a worthy companion will be available to you much sooner than it would be had you lived and died hundreds of years earlier!"

"That's true," she laughed. "I guess if I had been a contemporary of Columbus, I really would have had a long wait. All right, let me see if I understand all of this. I must do my best to find someone in this life, but if I am unable to do so, and I remain righteous and faithful to my covenants, I will have the opportunity to find a partner in the spirit world—with our sealing work to be performed during the Millennium."

"To me, that is what the Prophets seem to be saying," I said. "And you're right: the real issue is your faithfulness and obedience in this life to the commandments of the Lord. Then that choice will be open to you.

"Of course, if you *can* marry in mortality and be faithful, you have the potential of parenthood now and marriage in the spirit world too. You do not have to wait for the Millennium to be sealed to a companion." I shared with her these words from Elder Bruce R. McConkie: "We have the power to perform a marriage, and we can do it so that the man and the woman become husband and wife here and now and—if they keep the covenant there and then made—they will remain husband and wife in the spirit world and will come up in glory and dominion with kingdoms and exaltation in the resurrection, being husband

and wife and having eternal life. . . . That is our potential; that is within our possible realm of achievement." ("Celestial Marriage," in *1977 Devotional Speeches of the Year* [Provo, Utah: Brigham Young University Press, 1978], p. 172.)

Carol said, "So the advantage of being married now compared to finding a companion later is that as soon as both married people die and are together in the spirit world, they live as husband and wife in that sphere. Those who do not marry must await the Millennium, when their ordinance work will be completed for them."

"Yes, unless through our family research we can do that work now," I explained.

"All right," she said, "I see why I should keep trying to find a spouse, and I see why the Millennium is such an important period of temple work. Most people who have passed on to the spirit world must be anxious for that thousand-year period to begin so that they can obtain their sealings and qualify for eternal life."

"I think so. However, again, please don't resign yourself to that time frame," I reminded her. "There is still much that you can do to find a companion here."

"Apparently you haven't been out in the real world," she said with some cynicism.

"Maybe not," I said, "but who knows what will happen to you if you will do your part."

"What part can I do?"

"Well, I think that singles need to participate in activities where they can meet and get to know other singles. Whether single or married, we all need to be our best selves. I think you counsel with your Heavenly Father as to where you may find a companion and what you can do to prepare yourself. Establish relationships with other singles. Perhaps you could be a little more outgoing in seeking a companion. After all, faith without works is dead."

"Okay, okay. But at least Heavenly Father loves me after all, doesn't he," Carol said with a sigh.

"Of course he does. You are his daughter, and he wants you to have all the blessings to which you are entitled. As I see it, the marvelous plan that our Father prepared and presented to us in the Council in Heaven would be a cruel and unloving jest if he meant it to apply only to that tiny minority of men and women who have been married by priesthood authority during their mortal lives. I think that his very nature, expressed through the gospel plan, speaks otherwise. The Lord said that the gate is narrow and the way is strait, but no one is excluded who will walk the path of repentance, faith, and obedience. Nor are those excluded who were deprived in mortality of the opportunity to marry when they were not at fault, or where circumstances beyond their choosing or control prevented them from doing so."

Carol and I concluded by reading some comments from Elder M. Russell Ballard:

> A family can live with [God] only after a man and a woman are sealed in marriage for eternity by the power of the holy priesthood. We acknowledge that many in the Church desire this great blessing but see little evidence of its fulfillment in this life. Nevertheless, the promise of exaltation remains an attainable goal for each one of us. The prophets have stated clearly that no blessing will be withheld from any of God's sons and daughters if they love Him, have faith in Him, keep His commandments, and endure faithfully to the end.

Discussing men's and women's opportunities and responsibilities in relation to the family and God's plan, Elder Ballard went on to say:

> We need to recognize the hard mortal realities in all of this and must use common sense and guidance by personal revelation. Some will not marry in this life. Some marriages will fail. Some will not have children. Some children will choose not to respond to even the most devoted and careful nurturing by loving parents. . . . Let us not judge others, because we do not know their situation nor do we know what common sense and personal revelation have led them to do. We do know that throughout mortality, women and men will face challenges and tests of their commitment to God's plan for them. We need to remember that trials and temptations are an important part of our lives. ("Equality Through Diversity," *Ensign,* November 1993, p. 90.)

"What about being a parent?" Carol asked. "How will that work out?"

I responded by asking her to let me share with her one more quote from Elder Melvin J. Ballard:

> God bless those mothers who are not yet permitted through no fault of their own to be mothers in very deed, but who are nevertheless mothers at heart. The Lord looks upon the hearts of men and women, and their intent and they shall be judged according to their will and their desires. Such mothers shall not go through eternity childless. There are born into the world countless thousands of children who die in their infancy whose mothers unfortunately shall not go where these children shall be when, as little infants, they come up in the resurrection from the dead in their infant state to be, of necessity, under the care and direction of a loving mother until they grow to maturity; and no doubt worthy women who have not been granted the privilege of motherhood shall have their hearts satisfied in the adoption and in the eternal right and possession of these motherless children. So there is hope for all men and women who are unfortunate in this respect. (*Melvin J. Ballard: Crusader for Righteousness,* pp. 128–29.)

"Thanks," Carol said. "I think I've got it. This has given me hope. I'll do my best, and now I have something to look forward to, to cling to. I know that if I am righteous and keep my covenants, it is not 'if marriage and motherhood happen' but 'when they happen.'"

CHAPTER SIX

Finding an Eternal Companion

Mr. and Mrs. John Doe
are pleased to announce the marriage
of their daughter
Jill
to
William Smith Jr.
son of
Mr. and Mrs. William Smith.
The pleasure of your company is requested
at a celebration in their honor.

Each year we receive a number of wedding announcements inviting us to celebrate the union of a new couple. Two lovers are ready to pledge their lives to each other, and they invite family and friends to join them in an expression of their happiness.

At the same time we are congratulating the newlyweds, however, we learn of other couples who are breaking up, separating, or struggling to keep their marital ship afloat. Heartsick, we wonder what could possibly have led them to this decision. What causes two people to decide that they no longer want to go on as husband and wife? Why do they begin to divide children and assets as if they were so much property? The emotional suffering through the trauma of divorce is staggering. How does a great love story—they all begin that way, don't they?—turn into such a terrible nightmare, so that a husband and wife decide it is not worth continuing?

Before a couple marries, we often hear how compatible they are—how they met under unusual circumstances and seemed made for each other. Their courtship is clever and creative, and they spend abnormal amounts of time together doing things you wish you'd have thought to do in your courting days. Now that they are splitting up, however, we hear—usually from the same people—how immature, selfish, and unprepared the "other spouse" really was, and how obvious it was from the beginning that this match would never work! "We tried to warn them," comes the refrain, "but you know how kids are these days! They want it all now." Privately you muse, *What happened? They seemed so happy at the reception.*

Given our gospel perspective concerning the importance of marriage and family life and our understanding of its eternal significance, surely the heavens must weep along with disappointed parents and family members when a couple decides to sever their relationship and break covenants with their Heavenly Father. From a gospel perspective, the sobering part of divorce is that those who make this decision to terminate their marriages are admitting to God and to themselves that they cannot live the very plan that God ordained to exalt them. They are saying, in effect, that one or both of them is not sufficiently Christlike to make marriage work, or at least not *this* marriage. One or both partners are operating on a telestial or terrestrial level, and character changes must occur if the next marriage is to have a better outcome, or there may be no eternal marriage opportunity. Such opportunities are usually still possible. We see it frequently. Mental health and esteem can be restored. Sometimes a crisis like divorce can shock us, bring humility, and add valuable insights that cause us to change our attitude and perspective.

Divorce is generally a maturing process for those not prepared for marriage the first time. On the other hand, what does *anyone* know about marriage at eighteen, nineteen, twenty, twenty-one, twenty-two, twenty-three, and beyond? There must be a great deal of mercy extended to those who err but who will humble their hearts and learn from past mistakes. But can it not be said, gently if needed, that the person or persons responsible for breaking covenants and dissolving the marriage will have to explain those decisions and actions to the Great Judge who ordained marriage? Thankfully, the Lord is the one who makes those decisions.

What can we do to stem the stunning rate of marital instability? Actually, before a young couple jumps on the marriage bandwagon, there are a number of principles they might consider that will help to reduce the chances of their ending up in the proverbial ditch.

1. *Narrowing the success variables to those most likely to ensure happiness in marriage.* There are a few obvious qualifications Latter-day Saints should consider in a prospective mate. For example, has the husband served a mission? The normal age for male missionaries is between nineteen and twenty-five. What does it mean if a young man (not a convert but one who grows up in the Church) does not serve a mission? There may be some legitimate medical reasons that prevent missionary service, but in too many cases it indicates an insensitivity to spiritual promptings, a selfish streak that may still exist. Could any young man, for example, who grows up in the Church say, "You mean every young man is supposed to serve a mission? I never heard that before! Who said that?" I don't think so. Every young man in the Church has to come to grips with that obligation, and if a person decided not to serve, a fiancée needs to examine why. Was the reason justifiable? Or was it simply a lack of spirituality, a family situation, or inactivity? Most important, has the problem been corrected?

Another variable to consider is the history of Church activity—family home evening, seminary, institute, and so on—for both partners? Do both individuals have solid home backgrounds with parents who love each other and where there was a model of a strong, healthy marriage set before them? Exceptions to the ideal are certainly possible, but they need to be examined and not ignored.

Moral cleanliness is critical. Complete chastity before marriage is the standard, or sincere repentance for those who have erred. A worthy young man or young woman with a testimony of the Restoration, a love for the Book of Mormon and other scriptures, together with an appreciation for living prophets, may not guarantee a great marriage, but such a person is more likely to love God enough to obey righteous counsel, to be in harmony with the Lord's will, and to practice Christlike qualities.

Someone once said, "Take note of how your boyfriend treats his mother, for that is a good indication of how he will treat his wife." Similarly, President Ezra Taft Benson summarized what would be close to the ideal woman:

> Give me a young woman who loves home and family, who reads and ponders the scriptures daily, who has a burning testimony of the Book of Mormon. Give me a young woman who faithfully attends her church meetings, who is a seminary graduate, who has earned her Young Womanhood Recognition Award and wears it with pride! Give me a young woman who is virtuous and who has maintained her personal purity, who will not settle for less than a temple marriage, and I will give you a young woman who will perform miracles for the Lord now and throughout eternity. ("To the Young Women of the Church," *Ensign,* November 1986, p. 84.)

A comparable outline for the young man can be drawn up (see Ezra Taft Benson, "To the 'Youth of the Noble Birthright,'" *Ensign,* May 1986, p. 45). And when a mission is added to a young man's resume, there is a strong likelihood for his being a candidate for marital success.

Before settling into marriage, a person should not only be willing to date but also have had a variety of dating partners in order to experience the makeup of a wide range of personalities and potential partners. Before his mission a wise young man will date a number of girls to help him develop adequate social skills that he can employ as a missionary, yet he is to remain free to serve the Lord unencumbered. (Some carry this unencumbered business too far and are afraid to date at all!) One of my students wrote of her disappointment in her first years at the university:

My freshman and sophomore years were not good ones for me. I sat at home quite a bit. I had lots of guy friends and I thought I was pretty social, but the guys just liked me as a friend. What did I have to do to get a guy to like me? I have a pretty good self-esteem about myself. I'm not gorgeous, but I don't think I'm ugly. I dress decently. I think I have a pretty good wardrobe. I try to be a good member of the Church and have a testimony. Many of my friends and roommates have the same problem. We don't know what else to do. We've probably asked more guys out than have asked us out. It gets pretty frustrating.

Perhaps part of the problem is that most eighteen-year-old men are saving money for missions, and the twenty-one-year-old returned missionaries are too poor! However, friendships can be developed without formal and expensive outings. Group activities, family home evening sessions, firesides, long walks and talks—all are valuable, inexpensive ways to get acquainted and develop relationships. After a young man has served a mission and gained valuable spiritual training, he is more likely to select a companion who has similar values. A firm resolve to live the principles of the gospel will enhance the chances that any couple will have a successful marriage. Overlooking this major point is often the first mistake some people make in their mate selection.

2. *Combining emotions with good judgment.* A myth that pervades our society is that to succeed in marriage we must rely almost exclusively on feelings during the dating and getting-acquainted stages—what might be termed "chemistry." We are convinced that romantic feelings are the most authentic and important gauge of love after all, and we trust our feelings. We conclude that emotions are the most valid indicators of how well we will succeed in matching up with someone. But, in fact, feelings and emotions during dating may offer little real substance when it comes to predicting marital success. While emotions are important, they must be balanced with clear thinking. We have to ask ourselves some hard questions: Looking at our strengths, weaknesses, interests, and goals, are the two of us compatible? Do we have an excellent chance to succeed in our marriage because of similarities?

Deciding to marry because "I feel good about it" might be hard to argue against, but it might also represent a weak camouflage for sexual excitement, old-maid panic, or romantic fantasy. Feelings are not to be discounted, of course, but they must not be the sole criterion by which we judge the potential success of matrimony. There is always the danger in our culture of unduly romanticizing marriage and attributing to it unrealistic fantasies.

3. *Allowing time to get to know each other.* How disturbing to see a couple who have gone together only a few weeks claim surety that they know all they need to know about each other to enter into an eternal relationship! They think that after a brief courtship—during which they learned that they both like to dance and both like the same pizza toppings—surely they can handle whatever life throws at them. While there might be an occasional exception that succeeds, short courtships are most likely centered on infatuation, physical attraction, and superficial compatibility rather than a critical and wise assessment of one another's strengths and weaknesses. There must be sufficient time to observe how each one "wears" in a variety of situations, including being with your friends—his or her friends— and around each one's family. Marriage is for adults, and mature ones at that. Addressing his remarks to the single adult brethren of the Church, President Benson explained that "one good yardstick as to whether a person might be the right one for you is this: in her presence, do you think your noblest thoughts, do you aspire to your finest deeds, do you wish you were better than you are?" ("To the Single Adult Brethren of the Church," *Ensign,* May 1988, p. 53.) This usually requires a significant amount of interaction over an extended period of time.

Both partners need to consider a number of important issues before they are ready for the leap into marriage. A prospective mate's family background is more important than you might think when you are dating, for the older we become, the more we begin to look like our parents' clone. While it may seem that you marry only one other person, it turns out that you marry an entire family, an individual who is a composite of many generations. That may be your good fortune, or it may be a hidden mine field. (Of course, your partner has a similar risk in taking on your family! We tend to forget the other side.)

The early stages of dating and courtship tend to blind us to a potential spouse's weaknesses; similarly, we try to hide our own warts and blemishes as best we can. We want to appear perfect, and we easily ascribe perfection to the one causing our elevated pulse rate. It is easy to overlook character deficiencies during this romantic stage, because both are on their best behavior. Both are trying hard to be humorous, clever, and attractive, and yet appear down-to-earth. Many personality flaws can be hidden in courtship. Even marginal mental illness can be disguised during these exciting days!

Dating can cause a person to mask reality and obscure weaknesses—in some cases until the marriage is consummated. Sometimes it is not until we start living day in and day out with someone who does not share our cherished views that we question how carefully we made our marriage decision. Sometimes what we thought were strengths in a prospective mate later turn into liabilities. I am reminded of this little piece, which I adapted from something written by Sydney J. Harris:

Antics with Semantics

He married her because she seemed so pretty and petite; he divorced her because she was so weak and helpless.

She married him because he was such a strong personality; she divorced him because he was so domineering.

He married her because "she reminds me of my mother"; he divorced her because "she reminds me of *her* mother."

She married him because he was so ambitious, he was "going someplace"; she divorced him because he became a "workaholic."

He married her because "we were childhood sweethearts"; he divorced her because she "never grew up."

She married him because he was fun and romantic; she divorced him because he was shiftless and lazy.

He married her because she was "steady and sensible"; he divorced her because she was "dull and boring."

She married him because he was "sweet and attentive"; she divorced him because he was so possessive.

He married her because she was "such a beauty"; he divorced her because "all she thinks about is her looks."

She married him because he was so "intelligent and witty"; she divorced him because he was so "critical and wisecracking."

He married her because "we have such a great sexual attraction for each other"; he divorced her because "we have nothing in common anymore."

She married him because he was "the life of the party"; she divorced him because "he thinks life is just a party."

He married her because "she's so neat and clean"; he divorced her because "she thinks more of the furniture than she does me."

She married him because "we had such great talks together"; she divorced him because he's never home to talk anymore.

He married her because she had "such a gentle nature"; he divorced her because "she won't discipline the children."

She married him because "he swept me off my feet"; she divorced him because "he knocked me off my feet."

He married her because "she was so crazy about me"; he divorced her because she was so "insanely jealous."

She married him because he was the captain of the football team; she divorced him because she was a "football widow."

He married her because she was good with children; he divorced her because the children came before him.

She married him for his frugality and creative dating; she divorced him because he was such a tightwad!

One important character trait that needs close scrutiny before marriage is temperament, for temper can be the great destroyer of marriage and family relationships. Most of us have the ability to curb our tempers while dating, for we know that moodiness is not an attractive trait. It is not fun to be around temperamental people. Generally, anger is a technique to gain control over others or attention, a manipulative tool. Anger is a leading factor in most of the marital unhappiness preceding divorce. I've yet to see a friendly divorce!

A word about dating a person previously married: Sometimes those who divorce are anxious to remarry quickly in order to save face and portray to others that their breakup could not have been their fault. The "proof" lies in the fact that another person wants to marry them; hence they must be desirable. They intend to project the image that it must have been the ex-spouse who caused the first failure, for look how quickly someone else saw their attractiveness! Such rebounding usually has a disastrous outcome—often similar patterns that afflicted the first marriage recur in the second marriage—and if these individuals divorce a second time they tend to lose confidence in their ability to succeed in marriage. They can become soured on marriage. We must never lose faith in marriage.

On the other hand, some of the best marriages I've seen have been those where one partner got out of a difficult marriage and found a much more compatible spouse.

4. *Marrying within age limits.* Another important factor that influences marital stability is the "age at marriage" factor. Divorce statistics for those who marry under the age of twenty are extremely high and are a great concern to those who study the family. On the other end of the scale, people who marry in their late twenties and early thirties have difficulty maintaining a marriage also, perhaps due to the length of time they were single. Behavior patterns may be stubbornly set in concrete. Others become so comfortable in their single state that adjusting to a companion whose practices, ideas, habits, and decision-making processes are quite different is difficult. They can be inflexible on issues wherein they formerly had sole responsibility for the outcome. Before they marry, young men and women need a variety of dating and social experiences that will give them a maturity level needed to live and cooperate with another human being in the adventure of marriage and parenthood.

We can benefit from applying to our decisions the Lord's counsel to Oliver Cowdery: "Study it out in your mind; then you must ask me if it be right, and if it is right I will cause that your bosom shall burn within you; therefore, you shall feel that it is right. But if it be not right you shall have no such feelings, but you shall have a stupor of thought that shall cause you to forget the thing which is wrong." (D&C 9:8–9.) In order to study out in your mind the prospect of marrying someone, you must have adequate time to investigate important dimensions of your relationship. A confirmation of the Holy Ghost may speed, to some extent, the decision to marry by confirming that the relationship has possibilities, but we must not forget the admonition to do our own homework first. Such steps will help ensure that we won't find out too late that we are not as compatible as we presumed.

The Church missionary program comes to the rescue again to help resolve the problem of early marriage. Obviously a young man who faithfully serves a full-time mission for two years won't marry before age twenty-one, thereby providing much needed maturity. A mission helps a young elder or sister to be more grounded in faith and life experiences than he or she otherwise would have been without that seasoning. What an important role missions play in marriage preparation! Serving a mission allows a young person to learn how to deal with companion relations with a variety of personalities that begin in the Missionary Training Center and continue throughout a mission. These companions are chosen by the mission president, not the missionary; consequently, missionaries must, to a very real extent, deal with personalities different from their own and not of their own choice. What a great benefit that is to them before they begin their own mate selection! Later as they face marital differences, they already possess both a doctrinal perspective on marriage and experience in resolving differences with other personalities. Such a perspective and such experience can readily be applied in marriage relations, which in many ways can be quite similar to the companion relations that a mission presents. Missionaries learn that long talks, a spirit of cooperation, companionship inventories and evaluations, renewing commitments, fasting together, studying the gospel together, and expressing appreciation for each other enhances their companion relations—attitudes and practices that likewise can be invaluable in marriage relations.

A number of studies have shown that the length of time spent dating each other positively correlates to satisfaction in marriage. In other words, the longer a couple dates, the greater the odds are that both partners will rate their marriage satisfactorily. (Obviously, there is a limit to this. Engagements that last for years may indicate an inability to make commitments. Similarly, putting off marriage until certain educational or income levels are reached may be a socially approved way to avoid taking responsibility.) In general, however, the longer two people date, the better their chance to build a happy marriage. More specifically, statistics show that couples who "go together" for two years consistently rate higher on marital happiness than those who go together for a shorter time period. Missions may mature individuals sufficiently to reduce this time period.

Obviously, one danger of long courtships in our sex-oriented society is the temptation to stray beyond moral guidelines. A couple must be careful and prayerful to not put themselves in situations that are off-limits to singles. They need to discuss guidelines and limits. Each must be the guardian of the other's chastity, for both will yet be a mother or father of Heavenly Father's children. Longer courtships allow each to see a variety of personality variables and observe how each one functions in peer-group and family situations. We get a closer view of character traits like temper and humor in both formal and less formal settings. Most important, a person's spiritual depth and commitment to gospel principles cannot be hidden over a longer observation period.

5. *Reducing marriage anxiety.* Some are no doubt too opinionated in their search for the "perfect match." Others, because they know marriage is a requirement for exaltation, may become so anxious to marry that they ignore obvious differences. The danger is that some individuals focus on the "happily ever after" marriage myth itself rather than taking a good look at their own strengths and weaknesses and those of the person they intend to marry. While two people are enjoying a good time with one another in the dating phase, it is vital that they examine issues that will be important in marriage, such as power and control issues, decision-making patterns, manners, compatibility, attitudes concerning money management, sexual expectations, desire for children, work ethic, temperament, leisure-time activities, and religiosity.

Bill and Janet come to mind. She was twenty-six and he was twenty-two. That in and of itself was not the problem, particularly since women live longer than men, but it was obvious that Janet wanted this marriage to work because she was getting a little older, had not dated a great deal, and was worried that this might be her last opportunity. She was so anxious to be compatible that she minimized any differences with Bill. She answered for him, even though he was capable of speaking for himself. She wanted to pave the path with smooth stones by resolving any discrepancies that arose. She kept reassuring Bill that whatever his concerns were, they would be easier to resolve once they were married. She was sure that happiness came with the institution of marriage. Unfortunately, they married and it was soon obvious to Bill that being married to Janet was more like being married to a mother figure than to an equal partner. She needed to control the relationship. He felt smothered and unable to be himself.

Here is a general axiom: Getting married rarely solves problems; it usually accentuates them.

6. *Being committed to only each other.* A very confused young lady came into my office one day seeking help. She had accepted a ring and agreed to marry John, not because she was committed to him but because others had told her they were the perfect match. She liked John, but she was so unsure of herself that she was dating other young men with her wedding date little more than a week away! If either partner still desires to date others, they are certainly not ready for the commitment of marriage! Each individual must ask: Do I enjoy being with him or her? Are his or her needs as important to me as my own? Am I in love with him or her, or am I in love with love? Occasionally we talk ourselves into loving someone who our parents and friends think would be a wonderful spouse for us, but when it comes right down to it, we share little compatibility. You are the one who must live with this person, not your folks or friends.

In a discussion on choice and agency, the question always comes up, What about all those "arranged marriages" we read about historically and even currently in other cultures? If everything I have just said is true, how could arranged marriages possibly work? This is a legitimate question. Much could be said about arranged marriages, but the key factors that can make those marriages successful are missing today, at least in our society: cultural norms, respect for parental authority, commitment to the relationship, lack of opportunity to meet others, and nonacceptance of divorce as an escape hatch. They simply knew they had to make it work and they did. Today we seem to have a different set of rules.

This doesn't mean that you shouldn't pay attention to the advice of parents and friends. Perhaps they can be more objective about some things and may contribute observations on the relationship that you have missed, but a decision to marry someone else because of an admiration for their parents, home, lifestyle, earning power, education, upbringing and background, happy-go-lucky attitude, or social status may be a grave mistake. What you see is what you get, so look carefully.

7. *Looking deeper than external beauty and beyond sexual intimacy.* The prevailing theory in our society is that the more attractive or handsome a person is, the better spouse, parent, and lover he or she will be. What a dangerous premise! While a physically attractive person may very well have the depth and character you would like to have in a spouse, you certainly wouldn't want to depend on attraction as a gauge. We are easily blinded by physical appeal, and we assume that our emotional high is sufficient proof that all will be well between us. Such people assume that because the right chemistry is operating, all other problems will pale in comparison with the excitement of marital sex. The age-old question, "Can she cook?" and the casual response, "I don't know, but she's got a great body!" may get a laugh from the gang but can take on a new significance down the road when the honeymoon is over and the husband comes home hungry. The whole erroneous concept of "happily ever after" without effort comes from the Hollywood screen where homes are orderly, people always wear nice clothing, dating partners have plenty of money, and life is one big party. In the marriage clinic we see disillusioned couples who can't talk to each other, who have nothing in common beyond the bedroom, and actually had no idea who they married when they said "I do."

Some believe that sexual intimacy will solve any and all marital problems. "As long as we can sleep together," goes their rationale, "our marriage will be wonderful and any problems will easily be resolved." (Hollywood again.) However, couples soon learn this principle: the enjoyment of sexual intimacy is a reflection of the quality of the marriage as a whole; it is not a problem solver.

Like drink or dulling drugs, some view sex as an escape from reality. Following the excitement and release of sexual energy—or the bottle or drugs—the same problems still exist and need attention. No doubt physical endowments will always be important ingredients in our search for true love as long as the media portray most worthwhile people as thin, lithe, and gorgeous. "I admit," one of my students told me, "that I'm usually attracted to the gorgeous guys, the ones who have nice bodies and nice clothes. But these are the guys who, most of the time, have egos bigger than *they* are. The guys that I have actually dated in the past looked nothing like my ideal, but I was very happy when I was with them. These were guys I would actually consider marrying. Being out with a good-looking guy and having every girl's envy may seem like a good thing, but I'd rather be happy in the long run."

Of course, we should feel that our spouse is attractive and physically appealing. Romantic charisma is not unimportant. But soon after marriage it becomes obvious that other factors come center stage. An old saying that "hormones may get you into a marriage, but they will not keep you there" always brings to mind an even older one, "Beauty is only skin deep." People are not perfect; we are not all "10s." Sometimes perhaps we can be too picky about unimportant things. In his address to the single adult sisters of the Church, President Benson counseled:

> Do not expect perfection in your choice of a mate. Do not be so concerned about his physical appearance and his bank account that you overlook his more important qualities. Of course, he should be attractive to you, and he should be able to financially provide for you. But, does he have a strong testimony? Does he live the principles of the gospel and magnify his priesthood? Is he active in his ward and stake? Does he love home and family, and will he be a faithful husband and a good father? ("To the Single Adult Sisters of the Church," *Ensign,* November 1988, pp. 96–97.)

To the single men he recommended:

> Now, brethren, do not expect perfection in your choice of a mate. Do not be so particular that you overlook her most important qualities of having a strong testimony, living the principles of the gospel, loving home, wanting to be a mother in Zion, and supporting you in your priesthood responsibilities.
>
> Of course, she should be attractive to you, but do not just date one girl after another for the sole pleasure of dating without seeking the Lord's confirmation in your choice of your eternal companion. ("To the Single Adult Brethren of the Church," *Ensign,* May 1988, p. 53.)

In the next chapter we'll discuss how important healthy, intimate sexual relations can be in a marriage, but keep in mind that no matter how rewarding and therapeutic such relations in marriage are, the bedroom cannot be expected to hold up the structure of the entire marriage. Sometimes we are unable to have sexual relations (following delivery of a baby or during times of sickness and separation, for example), and we must have other interests and activities that meet our needs. The reality of life is that most of what we do in marriage is rather mundane and routine, and unless we enjoy talking and sharing ideas and feelings with each other, life in the bedroom will become shallow and routine.

8. *Living worthy of the Lord's guidance.* A final point to consider is how the Lord views your match. The Spirit of the Lord will enlighten your mind and help you to judge righteously, but he will not make the choice for you. God will not do anything for us that we can do for ourselves, is one of the principles of self-reliance and wisdom. He wants us to convince ourselves that we are making the very best decision we can and that we are going into this new relationship with our eyes open, having gained an appreciation for the qualities of the one we have chosen. We can receive a confirmation of a marriage partner, but it will come only, to use the words of Nephi's explanation of grace, "after all we can do" (2 Nephi 25:23).

Of course the difficulty comes in recognizing revelation and separating it from what you *want* the answer to be. You won't be sure unless you are familiar with the way the Spirit works with you from past experience. In other words, don't wait until this most important decision of your life to start experimenting with inspiration. If you grew up in the Church, you received the Holy Ghost at age eight. If you took advantage of opportunities, you have matured in your ability to recognize his still, small voice in your life—again the value of a mission is apparent.

A young woman came to my office one day and pleaded with me to tell her how to know for sure that this certain young man was the one the Lord would have her marry. She said she had some doubts about the relationship, and even though she had laid her concerns before the Lord, she was very confused about what she should do. When I visited further with her about her feelings and her personal experiences with the Lord as a counselor and guide, she admitted that she had never thought to turn to him in the past and had had no spiritual experience to draw from. As much as I wanted to put her out of her misery, I could only tell her what I have tried to convey in this chapter.

Even after you have done all you could do, marriage is, after all, a leap of faith. But please check out all the variables you can, the best you can, before you commit yourself to marriage.

Summary

By dating a person over a sufficiently long period of time, observing as many aspects of each other's life and personality as possible, becoming acquainted with each other's parents and background, and by using both heart and head, you can make the marriage decision wisely. As President Spencer W. Kimball expressed, "Certainly the most careful planning and thinking and praying and fasting should be done to be sure that of all decisions, this one is not wrong. In true marriage there must be a union of minds as well as of hearts. Emotions must not wholly determine decisions, but the mind and the heart, strengthened by fasting and prayer and serious consideration, will give one a maximum chance of marital happiness." (*The Teachings of Spencer W. Kimball*, ed. Edward L. Kimball [Salt Lake City: Bookcraft, 1982], p. 302.)

There is nothing as important as the creation of eternal family units. If we make good choices at the beginning of our relationship and remain true to our covenants and commitments, we can save ourselves a great deal of trouble later on. Our relationships can withstand the challenges of mortal testing, and we can, together, lay a foundation for an eternal companionship.

CHAPTER SEVEN

Marital Intimacy

Generally the quality of a marriage can be gauged by what happens in the bedroom. Very few husbands and wives can be angry and upset with each other and still enjoy this intimate side of marriage. Occasionally someone will say, "The only area where we *do* get along is in our sex life," but that is unusual. Marital intimacy is a fairly consistent barometer of how well a marriage is progressing, for if two people truly care for each other and look forward to these tender moments of touching and caressing, they already share a level of emotional acceptance sufficiently strong to resolve many of life's challenges.

The Purpose of Marital Intimacy

Our Heavenly Father designed sexual relations for married people for two primary reasons: to bring his children to mortality under the family umbrella, and as a way for them to express their feelings of love for each other in a significant way. Thus married partners renew their commitments and encourage each other to cooperate in fulfilling their marital roles. It is an important means for a couple to keep their matrimonial ship upright and afloat in life's sometimes treacherous and swirling current, a way to reaffirm their commitment to stay the course as they navigate their marital vessel through telestial channels.

Heavenly Father understood our need for an intimate, therapeutic relationship, and planted within us an attraction for each other that finds its consummation in the physical and emotional union of marriage. As couples we are brought back to our basic commitment and covenants. Our purpose and perspective are renewed, life is enriched, and we are reminded of our mutual dependence. Bearing children strengthens an already healthy bond between spouses through a strong incentive to stay together, for creating a mortal body is a most profound experience. This new creation provides a higher purpose and meaning as the parents share in an adventure that entails personal sacrifice, service, and caring for another human being.

Unfortunately, our worldly environment is hostile to marital commitments. It seems we are bombarded by immoral and degenerate messages. Sad to say, we live in a day when chastity and virtue are desecrated by men and women who attempt to profit from this divine attraction by portraying it as mere animal instinct. Paraded before our eyes by the media, unless we are wise enough to shut them out, are themes of promiscuity and adultery as if they were preferable to chastity and fidelity. When lewdness is treated so casually through a blatant disregard for decency, when women (future wives and mothers) are depicted as objects of sexual gratification, Christ-centered men and women are deeply offended. Madison Avenue, it seems, cannot present its messages without half-clothed bodies to pitch its products.

What a pathetic commentary it is that modern miracles such as television and motion pictures are used to procure money by converting wholesome desires and divine expressions of love between husband and wife into lust and lasciviousness for practically anyone—married or not! When so much good could be instilled in the young minds of this generation through positive role models, it is a shame that the immense power of these media so often tear away at chastity and virtue and undermine family values. Always, it seems, there are those foolish enough to listen and partake, thereby rewarding the purveyors and assuring a continuing stream of filth.

As Latter-day Saints, we are not automatically immune to this powerful propaganda, and Lucifer would love to persuade us, of all people, to partake of these materials, for he knows that immorality can prevent missions, temple marriages, and exaltation. He is aware that of the three most serious sins listed by Alma—denying the Holy Ghost, murder, and sexual immorality (see Alma 39:5)—his best chance of tripping up Latter-day Saints will be in this third category. Our greatest chance of losing exaltation is in the mockery of our sexual stewardship, for perhaps in this endowment, when used properly, we most imitate the heavenly pattern. "The plaguing sin of this generation is sexual immorality," President Ezra Taft Benson warned. "This, the Prophet Joseph said, would be the source of more temptations, more buffetings, and more difficulties for the elders of Israel than any other. . . . President Joseph F. Smith said that sexual impurity would be one of the three dangers that would threaten the Church within—and so it does. It permeates our society." (*The Teachings of Ezra Taft Benson* [Salt Lake City: Bookcraft, 1988], p. 277.)

Safeguarding Chastity

Every couple must preserve their relationship from the destructive seeds of immorality that blow about. We must not allow them to land, sprout, and overcome the good seed. Each spouse must remain true to his or her covenants and be aware of the importance chastity plays in underlying marital trust.

As couples, we are often hesitant to talk openly together about sexual intimacy, especially as newlyweds, because we do not have adequate terms to discuss our sexuality. Usually boys do not grow up talking to girls about female anatomy, and neither do girls talk to boys about male physiology. In fact, in marriage, one of our tasks is to learn (or create) terms that work well for us so that we can share clearly and comfortably our thoughts and feelings on this topic. We learn from each other arousal techniques that stir our sexual passion into an expression of our mutual feelings.

As companions, we need to share ideas and feelings on these matters, on occasion at least, or our marriages, like a car whose alignment needs attention, may hit a few potholes or brush up against the curbs of life and the result is not only jostled passengers but the threat that the vehicle could leave the pavement when we least suspect. President Spencer W. Kimball made the case more strongly: "If you study the divorces, as we have had to do in these past years, you will find there are one, two, three, four reasons. Generally sex is the first. They did not get along sexually. They may not say that in the court. They may not even tell that to their attorneys, but that is the reason." (*The Teachings of Spencer W. Kimball,* ed. Edward L. Kimball [Salt Lake City: Bookcraft, 1982], p. 312.)

Sexual Intimacy as Therapy

Sexual intimacy is an important form of marital therapy. I have written elsewhere: "Marriage is not just for sex, of course, but sex *is* a profound means of expressing love and commitment. It is designed to be a physical, emotional, and spiritual union. . . . Just as a good marriage increases sexual ardor, so satisfactory sexual relations add soul-binding strength to the marriage. There are few ways as powerful as the sexual union of a man and woman to express affection and romantic love. By shutting out the world, a couple, in the intimacy and privacy of their own room, can renew their vows and pledge of fidelity." (*Toward a Celestial Marriage* [Salt Lake City: Bookcraft, 1986], p. 141.)

I have talked to couples who have gone years without this physical and emotional therapy. What an enormous loss it has been to their souls and to their spirituality! How refreshing and renewing, how relaxing and wholesome is this privilege for married people, under immense pressures of work, marriage, and parenting responsibilities, to be reassured that they are desirable and needed!

Through their intimate contact, married couples can shut out worldly distractions, and in their own private space renew their marital commitments. The two halves are again whole. Two partners pledge themselves to their most important cause—a celestial family. Sharing physically and emotionally confirms each one's desirability and enhances the overall quality of the marriage. Too, a good marriage strengthens our mental and emotional health. Where communication is unrestricted, consistent, and honest, and each partner responsibly fulfills his or her marital roles, intimate relationships become a dynamic way to say "Thanks for being my companion" and "Thanks for allowing me to walk with you the path to exaltation."

In contrast, when a husband and wife have marital problems, the desire to share and cooperate is suppressed, if not eliminated. When feelings are trampled, motives impugned, and efforts unacknowledged and unappreciated, sexual relations bring little enjoyment, and perhaps even some dishonesty can exist in this area when inwardly hearts do not mesh. No person wants to share heart and soul with one who will not or does not appreciate the gift or who is critical of the giver. To "have sex" when the relationship is strained reduces this divine drama to a duty, a chore, and a drudgery in which neither participant appreciates its sublime grace and beauty.

"Sometimes I feel like a prostitute in my own home," a disappointed bride of three years told me. "I have a hard time wanting to participate in any intimacy when my husband snarls and gripes about all the things that I do wrong, and then he expects me to be ready at his beck and call."

Intimacy is a right and a privilege in marriage. The first time I thought of marital intimacy as a right was many years ago in a class I was teaching. Each person took a turn introducing himself or herself, sharing background information so we could all get acquainted. One student indicated that she had been married, but something had happened. I asked her to stay after class for a minute.

"Sandra, how did you go from a temple marriage to a divorce in only seven months?" I asked rather pointedly.

"Well, after my husband and I were married, we never had sexual relations," she replied.

"Would you mind explaining that?" I asked.

"He simply wasn't interested," she responded. "It turned out that he was homosexual and wanted nothing to do with me; so, I got an annulment."

She received an annulment and a cancellation of sealing

because in both civil law and gospel law, an important element of the marriage contract holds the expectation that sexual relations will be a part of every marriage. When that was not possible for her, she obtained an annulment.

The privilege of sexual relations implies that though two people may be legally married, intimacy cannot be forced, coerced, demanded, or be conditional. It is a proper expression of love between a husband and a wife, not a means to exploit one's spouse or simply satisfy one's selfish cravings.

Men, Women, and Sexual Intimacy

Men and women have different makeups, and despite a danger in stereotyping, some points are worth consideration. Men and women enjoy sexual intimacy, of course, because it is physically and emotionally stimulating; in short, it makes us feel good. We are housed in bodies of flesh and blood. We receive pleasure from physical stimulation—back rubs, massages, strokes, and gentle caresses. The love act's culmination—orgasm—can be a strong and pleasant sensation for both husbands and wives, a relief of sexual tension that originates from physical foreplay and sexual intercourse.

Though not essential to maintain life, marital intimacy resembles an appetite—much like our need for food—a drive or urge that makes it very much worth repeating, regularly. We look forward to this union. Marriage legitimizes a relationship forbidden by the Lord until marriage, and premarital standards of chastity and abstinence probably heighten our anticipation and pleasure.

During the honeymoon period, sexual intimacy is somewhat of a novelty, a newfound avenue to express the love and affection as well as the commitment we developed during our courting stages. Each person becomes aware of his or her own arousal states and physical sensations as the couple settle into a comfortable frequency and learn from each other techniques that work well. Both husband and wife must teach each other their respective preferences and approaches to arousal. Sexual intimacy can easily become a selfish quest for men because of the consistency of their drive for pleasure. As a husband matures in his spirituality, however, he becomes more charitable and considerate of his wife's feelings and he can regulate his sexual desires to be compatible with hers. His willingness to please her increases so that her sexual fulfillment becomes the center of his enjoyment. The same is true for her. The memories of previous intimate interludes increase their desire to repeat the pleasures of conjugality.

Most important, couples need to make sure that sexual intimacy does not become a boring or routine performance for either spouse, a battleground for resolving marital issues, a pawn to control the relationship, or a selfish attempt to receive personal gratification without regard for the feelings of the spouse. Too, both partners should be sensitive to the fact that sexual relations are designed to be therapeutic and can, for example, help a spouse to recover from a rough day. Marital intimacy is also a way to say hello to one's companion following an absence, or a means to spice up the relationship. Even when one is tired or exhausted but the need is evident, charity may require either spouse to go the extra mile to accommodate the other, with an appropriate expression of appreciation for any sacrifice on a spouse's part. We share more freely when we are loved and appreciated and our spouse is striving to fulfill his or her part of the marriage. We must know that there are times when only this form of therapy will do and that we can't always gauge our partner's interest by our own.

Male Sexual Arousal

The following would not be an unusual pattern: a husband decides (especially if a few days have passed since the last experience) that he would like to be intimate with his spouse that evening. His decision at this point has nothing to do with his wife's feelings. He arrives home, and either consciously or unconsciously he assumes that his wife feels the same way he does and that at the appropriate time she will guess what's on his mind. If she guesses right, the scenario takes place as he envisioned it would, and he is reinforced in his approach. After all, we repeat behavior that is personally rewarding and fulfilling.

If the scenario does not unfold as he visualized it would, he may become frustrated and perhaps irritated. If he is immature, he may push for sex despite the fact that his wife's feelings or schedule may preclude her interest or willingness to respond as he would like. Most husbands handle this disappointment well if it is sporadic. But if it becomes a pattern in the marriage, and he is rebuffed consistently, he begins to go through a series of mental gyrations to explain what is going on. Here he is married, enjoys lovemaking, and should be having frequent sexual relations; yet, his wife is not cooperating! Often he will not openly discuss his frustration, but he privately fumes or tries again at a later time. If he is repeatedly rejected, he may punish his wife in return by not talking, being irritable (but denying it), or using some other technique that has worked for him in the past.

Of course, a better route would be to investigate her feelings, check the relationship, evaluate the marriage, and find out from her what is going on between the two of them. Sometimes the reasons for her apparent lack of interest are simply physiological, a temporary situation in which lovemaking would be physically uncomfortable; or perhaps her expectations for frequency do not match his. Most couples could write a book on the miscommunication that occurs in their efforts to mesh their sexual desires and appetites.

Time affects our sexual desire and energy. Beginning with the honeymoon, during which time intimacy is probably a daily event, most young husbands would enjoy sexual intercourse daily, but as with any appetite, self-restraint best preserves its freshness and novelty. The principle here is analogous to that recognized by the fast-food lover whose steady diet of Big Macs eventually diminishes any cravings he has for that food.

Too, selfishness can rear its ugly head, without being obvious, because marriage is supposed to be the place for sexual privilege. Without regard for their spouses interests and feelings, many men presume sex to be available on demand. Professions of love as a prelude to sexual intimacy can become a manipulative tool for personal gratification.

Surveys among happily married men reflect a high frequency of sexual intercourse. Sexual relations should be mutually agreeable and not simply a husband's right. Every wife has a right to participate and enjoy her own sexual fulfillment. "Husband and wife . . . are authorized, in fact they are commanded, to have proper sex when they are properly married for time and eternity," said President Spencer W. Kimball. "That does not mean that we need to go to great extremes. That does not mean that a woman is the servant of her husband. It does not mean that any man has a right to demand sex anytime that he might want it. He should be reasonable and understanding and it should be a general program between the two, so they understand and everybody is happy about it." (*The Teachings of Spencer W. Kimball,* ed. Edward L. Kimball [Salt Lake City: Bookcraft, 1982], p. 312.)

"My husband has no interest in how I feel about our relationship," Sally fumed, "or how the day has gone *for me.* He just wants to jump into bed and satisfy his needs. Has he thought about me for two seconds and how I feel? Sometimes I am so upset with him and he is totally unconscious; he doesn't even know I'm angry. After wrestling with the kids all day, changing diapers, or scrubbing floors and bathrooms, I am not feeling very lovable or sexy, especially when he comes in the door griping about the condition of the house or when he pays no attention to me or the kids on the way through. At times like that I feel exploited, used—like I have no say in the marriage except to be at his beck and call. Sometimes I feel that when he goes on a business trip, the only reason he wants me to go along is so he can have a sex partner. And then, instead of my enjoying sex, it becomes a duty, and then I hate it. He never asks me if I enjoy it, or if I am satisfied. I wish he would get a clue!"

Every husband should learn this lesson early in marriage: romance is not something that occurs a few minutes before sex takes place; it should be a way of life that makes a wife feel loved and appreciated continually for her contribution to the success of the marriage. Talking, sharing nonsexual affection, and consistent validation are helpful keys to a wife's interest and enthusiasm for sexual contact—this, combined with sexual techniques that meet her needs for sexual fulfillment. Occasionally I hear a wife say, "The only time my husband tells me that he loves me is when we are being intimate." If a wife hears expressions of love only during sexual intercourse, she would no doubt be a little suspicious that her husband doesn't love her as much as he loves the personal gratification he receives.

To selfish men, abstinence during a wife's menstrual period becomes a time for cynicism. "When will you be through with the curse?" he may rudely ask. "Are you ever going to be through with this female thing?" The message the wife receives is, "You are doing this on purpose. Hurry up so you can service my needs." This is hurtful to a wife, for she is being criticized for that which makes her female. After all, if she didn't ovulate, she could not become a mother. And what righteous husband would not want to be a father? Some husbands seem determined to have sexual relations regardless of her health, comfort, or convenience. (Of course, a wife who uses health as an excuse for extensive abstinence might cause her husband to question if there is more than a physical problem.)

A wife will need rest from the conditions and responsibilities associated with her role, such as those of nursing, being up at night with sick children, enduring pregnancy, feeling exhausted, having her menstrual cycle, or passing through menopause. A husband's charity must stretch wide enough to be considerate of his wife's feelings and health; he will not push for sexual intimacy when it is obviously not appropriate or appealing to her.

There are times when a wife may not respond as enthusiastically to her husband's advances as he would like. Likewise, there are times when orgasm is not her goal. Should her husband continue to try to arouse her, it can irritate her physically and emotionally. Sometimes simply lying next to each other, side by side, with quiet touches can be deeply satisfying. Women enjoy hugs, kisses, and nonsexual affection. At other times, full passion may bloom into an ecstasy that will surprise both companions. The point is that you must teach each other what is enjoyable and fulfilling for you so that each of you may gain from this relationship what the Creator intended. We need to be sensitive to moods and feelings. Women are often willing to share themselves even when they are tired from their heavy responsibilities. And a husband must be aware that even though he might feel "turned on," if his wife has had a frustrating day, she may not be in the mood for sexual relations.

Conversely, sacrifice is a part of every marriage, and because sexual relations are generally therapeutic to one or both spouses, marital intimacy can be an opportunity for each to fill this role as necessary to meet a spouse's needs for reassurance, comfort, stimulation, and renewal. A woman who keeps an "accounting ledger," so that begging and cajoling by her husband is necessary to receive a pittance and miserly dispensing of sexual favors is the rule, will drive a wedge between the two—a circumstance which, on occasion, becomes an excuse for an affair. Alternately, some women receive far too little sexual support and attention from their husbands and would like an increase in sexual play. Under such circumstances, the husband needs to be more attentive to meet her needs. More and more I hear from wives that *they* would enjoy more sexual relations. Knowing how your spouse feels about frequency and sexual techniques is essential for both companions if intimacy is to fulfill its purposes in their marriage. The best source of information is each other, for who else knows of your individual preferences and desires?

Now, a word or two about male sexual response: Following intercourse, husbands lose their sexual passion almost immediately and are unable to be sexually aroused again for a period of time. Younger husbands may be physically aroused again in hours, whereas older husbands may require a day or two to recover their potency. But a wife has a telltale sign that her husband is physically aroused because of his erection. As a man ages and loses testosterone or develops physical limitations, it is important for a wife to know this so that she may assist him to an arousal state, perhaps through more physical stimulation than was needed earlier in their marriage. Or she may reassure him that being close and intimate is more important to her at the moment than intercourse. After a period of abstinence, male sexual libido usually rises and his normal sexual energy returns. Again, the length of time required for this cycle depends on his age and physical stamina.

As to the frequency of sexual intimacy, generally married couples who are beyond the honeymoon years settle in to two to three times each week until they pass menopause, when their frequency may diminish to once a week or less.

Men, even if they have put in a day of strenuous physical labor, usually find lovemaking to be relaxing and therapeutic. Seeing a wife change into her nightgown or pajamas is sufficient to cause a rise in his sexual desire for her. Men tend to equate love and sex. If his wife is willing to participate with him in this powerful experience, a man thinks, she must love him! His need for affection and touch are also met in an overwhelming expression of love for her. This is a strong driving mechanism in most men that leads them to seek frequent sexual relations.

A wife may misinterpret her husband's desire for lovemaking as selfish. But because men feel an intense emotion at the time of climax, it is easy to interpret this as love; and indeed, to him it is love. It may very well be his way of expressing directly, "I love you," though it is more easily said physically than verbally.

Female Sexual Arousal

Generally, a wife is a little more complicated in her sexual interest and responses than is her husband, and perhaps a little more discriminating too! She, of course, likes to look at a handsome, masculine husband, but her sexual interest and arousal are generally more attuned to how she feels about her companion's attitude and approach to marriage, his skill and desire relative to being a father, and his overall competency as a spouse. A husband may be under stress all day, have a fight with his boss, get detained in traffic, and run over the dog in the driveway, but he can come home ready for sexual intimacy. His wife, on the other hand, may be quite different. Unless she feels valued and loved and respected in all of the nonsexual areas of marriage, she might find it difficult to participate in sexual relations without some resentment. If she feels neglected or is disappointed in his family leadership, if she feels he is distant and aloof or is critical of her efforts at homemaking or motherhood, she will find sharing herself physically and emotionally to be difficult. Unless he is the man he ought to be—exemplifying Christlike traits, being tender and loving and communicative, reaching out to meet her needs and touching her life positively—intimacy might repel her.

All of this is apart from physical attractiveness. Women often better tolerate physical defects in a spouse than do men. How a man carries out his marital roles and how well he conveys to his wife that she is his first priority are more important to her peace of mind and her ability to enjoy sexual relations than anything to do with his physical endowments. For wives, sexual intimacy is more likely connected to general feelings about the quality of the marriage than any other factor. Anatomically a wife has a greater capacity for sex; however, whether she enjoys this intimate association with her husband depends largely on his gentleness and sensitivity to her and the children.

On the other hand, a wife can also destroy romance for her husband if she criticizes him on his abilities. We all have a fear of rejection, of not measuring up to a spouse's expectations. In that regard, men and women are similar.

A wife can have a hard time putting out of her mind household and family worries—Is the stove turned off? Why is Billy coughing? When will I find time to prepare my Sunday School lesson? Does he have an ironed shirt ready for tomorrow? She may mentally review each of these topics before she can concentrate on sexual matters. Husbands do not usually run through such checklists. In fact, a husband might be disappointed to find his wife not focusing on the moment. May I suggest, husband, that you pass it off as insignificant to the quality of your sexual relations—it comes with motherhood! Be grateful that she is so conscientious about your home and your children. (If it happens all the time, you might want to take time out for a good discussion of what is going on in the marriage and how you feel it affects your intimate relations.)

Occasionally a mother is so exhausted from supervising her own brood—plus the neighborhood's—that she is asleep as soon as her head hits the pillow. Perhaps every wife needs to reassure her husband periodically, "Honey, there are times when I have a hard time concentrating. I am so tired after a day of chasing the kids around that I can hardly keep my eyes open. But that doesn't mean that I don't love you, or that I don't enjoy being close to you, or that I mind at all sharing this important time with you. Just wake me up if I go to sleep."

Increasing Sexual Enjoyment

Couples can engage in a variety of sexual play at different times of the day and in places other than the bedroom. Various erotic approaches can create spontaneity and pleasure for both partners in ways that are dignified, enjoyable, and still within the bounds of propriety.

It is also important that both partners are hygienically prepared, with no unpleasant odors to hinder romance. (Sometimes dental flossing, brushing, and mouthwash can help; showers, shampoos, and perfume or cologne can add additional romantic aromas and scents.) You want to be your best self at this close range.

A husband and a wife must be sensitive to the other's body and feelings about that body. Feelings of modesty and intimacy are very closely tied to how we see ourselves and evaluate our self-worth. Comments that diminish or lower a wife's self-valuation influence how she functions as a lover, wife, and mother. Cutting and hurting remarks are not easily forgotten—or forgiven. A husband's disparaging remarks about the size of her breasts, the shape of her legs, the frequency and length of her periods, her freckles or moles, or her body shape, for example, may stay in her mind and heart and inhibit her lovemaking. The same is true for men. We all seem to recall criticism much longer than we remember compliments. We can often easily call back such remarks—even though they were made years ago, and in jest at that. We may harbor the belief that there must have been some truth behind the statement or it would not have been said. There are few things more devastating than an attack on our physical endowments; besides, there is little we can do to change or enhance these traits.

Sexual intercourse needs to be preceded by kind and tender communication, by caressing and gentle sharing of mind and body. It is important that husbands and wives teach each other how to give and receive love. No two people are the same or have the same exact needs. Many wives, for example, do not like a great deal of manual stimulation of their genital area, but some do—if it is gentle and tender. Some would prefer other erotic areas of their bodies to be touched and caressed. A good foot rub, a neck or back rub, a scalp massage, or the careful stroking and kissing of the mouth and breasts are usually a more important prelude to a wife's sexual arousal than direct genital touch and stimulation. Unlike her, however, a husband may prefer gentle but direct touching and caressing of his genitals, for that is often the most intense foreplay for him. Each companion must take the responsibility to share with the other what is most enjoyable and relaxing as a part of his or her personal sexual fulfillment.

Without question, frequent and healthy sexual relations are an important part of a stable marriage. As a means of communication and therapy unlike any other, this relationship becomes a way in which two covenant people can express in powerful ways—physically, spiritually, and emotionally—their love and commitment to marriage and to each other. With this expression of oneness, they are able to overlook mutual weaknesses and mistakes. The message that we love each other comes through so strongly through intimate expressions that we overlook faults and failings. Satisfaction of our sexual needs can compensate for our inadequacies in other areas of the marriage.

Sexual intimacy is a cement that binds two married people together, renews their commitment to continue as a couple and family down unknown paths, provides a way to express mutual feelings of love and satisfaction, and fuels a love that can then extend out through all our interactions. The personal validation and feelings exchanged through such intimacy enable both spouses to proceed through the inevitable rough spots of parenting and all the mundane projects they must complete.

On the other hand, when we are angry, critical, or accusing each other of not holding up family responsibilities, we quickly learn that sexual relations are not enjoyable and we avoid them. No one wants to give himself or herself to a partner who is unappreciative or insensitive to the best gift you can give—yourself. Without the tender moments that can be ours through an intimate expression of love, marriage soon loses its attraction and fails to fulfill our most basic needs. These conditions attract the parasites of adultery and affairs that feed upon troubled marriage relationships. President Kimball said that selfishness is at the root of all divorce, and nowhere is this more obvious than in the bedroom, where selfish demands or rights are sometimes asserted.

Couples who are not sharing physical love frequently are usually starving emotionally. When couples die emotionally, it is because each is not receiving the nourishment that comes from being loved, wanted, needed, and cherished by a companion.

Such strong personal needs can be met only in the intimate consummation of marriage. The love we have for our children is a different kind of love, and even though they return love, it is of a different kind. Sex for the sake of sex doesn't do it either. There is little pleasure to be found in intimate relations when the marriage is lacking in genuine love and honest expressions of appreciation and adoration for one another.

Sexual Dysfunction

Men and women may differ in their rate of sexual arousal. In general, men are more easily aroused sexually than women. Without more open communication, a wife's sexual arousal may not be as obvious to her husband as his is to her; she may need to be more communicative as to her stages of arousal.

A husband's reaching a climax before his wife is sexually aroused—an occurrence often referred to as premature ejaculation—is a common marital problem. There are several reasons for this. A husband may misinterpret his wife's state of arousal and think she is nearing a climax, which increases his excitement so that he completes his own cycle before she nears her own orgastic phase. If a substantial interval has passed since their last sexual interlude, the husband, in his arousal, may be unable to control his timing. Sometimes the wife has just begun to focus on her own arousal state when her husband has already finished his. Thus she is left unfulfilled and frustrated.

Another time an early orgasm may occur for a husband is if he has had problems attaining or maintaining his own sexual arousal and this has increased his anxiety level. Anxiety about attaining or maintaining his libido seems to be connected to his own inability to function. The only time he has an erection in this case is just before climax, and that is followed by a cessation of his ability to continue intercourse. Generally it is embarrassing for a husband to be unable to attain or maintain an erection, for an ability to do so is an expectation of both him and his wife and is essentially necessary for intercourse. The paradox is that the more he thinks about it at the time when he wants to perform, the more he may be unable to reach it. If a husband is struggling with his own functionality, he needs to share that information with his wife so that she can either help with more physical stimulation or understand his dilemma. She needs to realize that it has nothing to do with his love for her; it is simply that his body will not carry out his demands.

The danger is that if a husband becomes obsessed with his inability to become sexually aroused, he may fear sexual intimacy with his wife and look for ways to avoid further embarrassment. For a man, there are few fears worse than the fear of being unable to function sexually. When he loses confidence in this ability (and sometimes the problem is traceable to medicines that inhibit his sex drive), he despairs. Then he may avoid sexual relations, which confuses his wife, who concludes that she is unattractive or undesirable to him, when that is not the case at all. Instead of trying to escape through television, dishes, work in the garage or yard until it is too late to snuggle or both are too tired, a husband should initiate a good discussion with her on his sexual functioning. That is one reason why helping each other to understand physical changes affecting sexuality is so important. When both spouses are aware of physical limitations, not only can embarrassment be avoided but each can help the other to meet needs for touching and intimacy that may not include sexual intercourse. A wife can help her husband with more manual stimulation, if that works, and he can be more attentive to her physical needs for affection.

It is interesting to note that as a man ages, sexual relations are good physical therapy for his prostate gland and may improve his chances for avoiding cancer.

Other problems can occur if a husband consistently moves through the arousal cycle to climax before his wife is sexually aroused. Her own sexual needs may never be satisfied, and so she might begin to invent excuses for not going to bed when he does, or she might find other rewarding activities in order to avoid the frustration of sexual relations. Again, the need for honest, open (yet tactful) discussion in resolving such problems becomes apparent.

A number of women do not experience orgasm, or at least they may do so only infrequently. This may be due to several factors, such as genetic makeup (perhaps 10 percent of women are inorgasmic), a fear of pregnancy, or a fear of sexual relations that stems from possibly years of negative information about sex. "It is just something that you have to tolerate as a woman," some disgruntled wives may tell a newlywed. Too, as a church, we strongly teach, and rightly so, abstinence before marriage and consider premarital sex a serious sin. Both sexes attend a number of "standards nights" during their Mutual years before they come to the marriage altar. Missionaries spend eighteen months to two years as "monks" shutting down all sexual drives. Suddenly these individuals are expected to lose all of their inhibitions because they are married. In a matter of hours, it is assumed that they can throw a mental switch and suddenly be aggressive in a sexual way. One day, sex was totally off limits; the next, it is both legal and expected. For many this is an easy transition, but for some it is not.

Some women are not orgastic because of their husbands' techniques or hygiene. After his own sexual release, for example, a husband feels contented and may go to sleep, possibly leaving his wife feeling frustrated at being half-aroused at best or feeling used and exploited at worst. She might interpret his actions as selfish and therefore resent him. A husband would do well to learn from his wife how to meet her sexual needs more explicitly so she can move through the same cycle of arousal, plateau, orgasm, and resolution together. This will require charity, self-control, lots of teaching and sharing, and practice. There will be times when one or the other will not care about the complete cycle and will be satisfied with fulfilling his or her spouse without concentrating on an orgasm. Those times will be known only if the two are communicating their feelings—usually at other times than in the heat of passion.

As men age, the tables may reverse. A wife might anticipate more sexual intimacy, particularly as she passes childbearing age and the complications of pregnancy are lessened. If her husband watches sports on television until late hours, falling asleep in front of the tube, she will be frustrated. As one woman told me, "The sports page gets more fondling than I do." Husbands who are sports or garden or garage buffs, please wake up and be aware of your companions' needs. "Many of us enjoy going to ball games and watching them on television," said Elder Joseph B. Wirthlin. "I am no exception. I love to watch a good athletic contest. If we spend excessive time with sporting events, however, we may neglect things that are much more important." (In Conference Report, October 1990, p. 81.)

Expressions of love must be freewill offerings from spouse to spouse. They cannot be forced, embarrassing, or immodest. Such expressions of love must be sensitive and indicate an understanding of each other's private world of chastity and modesty. Without knowing each other's needs, we may develop patterns of relating that are frustrating rather than helpful.

Here is a typical pattern in unhappy marriages: Anger and frustration (over sex, money, discipline of children—the topic doesn't matter) lead a husband to say unkind things to his wife. She does not feel like sharing herself with her critical husband, so she avoids sexual contact with him. This avoidance makes him even more angry and irritable, which causes her to want even less intimacy, and the pattern continues. This is a very common scenario in many marriages. The worst case I ever encountered was a couple who went more than ten years without sexual relations. What a barren wasteland! I asked them, "Do you two live in the same city? on the same block? in the same house? Do you sleep in the same room? the same bed?" They answered yes to all of these. Finally I blurted out, "Don't you ever run into each other?" It is this negative pattern that President Kimball spotted and labeled as so dangerous in marriage.

Summary

Sexual intimacy was designed by our Maker not only to provide bodies for spirits entering mortality but also to allow a man and a wife an important means of expressing love, appreciation, and mutual caring. When the need for physical intimacy is not met on a consistent, ongoing basis, emotions and feelings begin to wane. Then two frustrated marriage partners begin to look for the source of the problem, and unfortunately each usually concludes that the fault lies with the other—an attitude which can become a poison that spreads to other areas of the marriage.

The key to sexual satisfaction in marriage stems from the way each partner meets the needs of the spouse in the nonsexual areas of marriage. Intimacy is simply an extension of an already healthy marriage. Communication and gentle instruction and learning from each other help us find pleasure and satisfaction in our intimate experiences. In this way we can develop sexual habits and techniques that enable us to fulfill our individual sexual needs, thus creating a therapeutic environment in which marriage may blossom. We thereby more nearly approach our divine potential.

CHAPTER EIGHT

Selfishness and Pride—The Twin Plagues of Our Day

The Lord has poured out his Spirit in these latter days, as Joel predicted (see Joel 2:28–29). We have been blessed with unbelievable inventions and technology that have made our lives comfortable. Can you imagine trying to explain a computer to the pioneers, or modern automobiles, fax machines, or cordless phones, or how airplanes can cover in a little over an hour the same distance that took them months to cross? How blessed we are to live in these days of marvelous inventions that are the fruits of modern scientific truths!

Other truths that affect our lives are spiritual truths that come to us from God through revelation to his prophets. These truths are of a different kind than scientific truths, for we cannot see or measure them in the same way. For example, in this life you probably have never seen Satan, Adam and Eve, the celestial kingdom, the spirit world, the brass plates, the Urim and Thummim, the Savior, angels, or the Judgment Day, but you probably believe in their existence, because God has revealed a knowledge of them through his servants. These truths are the objects of faith, "things hoped for, the evidence of things not seen" but which are true, as Paul declared (Hebrews 11:1; see also Alma 32:21).

The prophets who reveal these truths are not located on mountaintops or in ivory towers. They are married men, fathers, and grandfathers. They grow up among us and are familiar with the wide range of human nature and behavior. By the time a man becomes the senior Apostle and President of the Church, he has traveled extensively, spoken with thousands of people, and matured in the endowments of the Spirit so that he knows both the will of God and the hearts and minds of men. Prophets, by virtue of their calling and experience, have inspired insights on the plan of salvation and an understanding of the acts of men and women. This has been repeatedly confirmed to me as I have taught a course entitled "The Teachings of the Living Prophets" almost every year of my teaching career.

In 1975, after I had completed graduate work in an excellent program, I heard a prophet of the Lord, President Spencer W. Kimball, declare: "Every divorce is the result of selfishness on the part of one or the other or both parties to a marriage contract. Someone is thinking of self-comforts, conveniences, freedoms, luxuries, or ease." (*The Teachings of Spencer W. Kimball,* ed. Edward L. Kimball [Salt Lake City: Bookcraft, 1982], p. 313.) The term "every divorce" caught my attention, because it was a strong signal that the old Nephite diseases of pride and selfishness were at work in this modern era—and a prophet was labeling selfishness as *the* major cause of divorce. It is different from the variables I studied in graduate school, such as socioeconomic status, sexual compatibility, spouse's employment, power and control issues, socialization, religiosity, age at marriage, in-law problems, interracial marriage, role incompatibility, role discrepancies, and a host of others. I could recall no formal studies on selfishness, yet here was a prophet ascribing marital instability to this trait.

Now, after years of closely observing divorce and interviewing and teaching many who have split up, I believe President Kimball's statement to be true—profoundly true.

Years after the prophet's remarks, his successor, President

Ezra Taft Benson, outlined the dangers of pride, a negative term in all scriptural contexts. He viewed selfishness as a major component of pride. In retrospect, then, these last two prophets, in training their prophetic eyes on marriage and divorce in the 1970s, '80s and '90s, have concluded that individual selfishness and overall pride are among the most common causes of marital breakdowns. Therefore, each of us must look carefully at our own lives to ensure that we are avoiding these two deadly viruses.

When we analyze the many faces of pride, we can easily see their virulent implications. If we can understand how their tentacles can wrap themselves around us, perhaps we can save a number of marriages that otherwise would be strangled in their grasp. In his seminal address on pride, President Benson said a central feature of this classic Nephite sin was "enmity toward God" and "enmity toward our fellowmen" (in Conference Report, April 1989, p. 3). He explained, "This message has been weighing heavily on my soul for some time. I know the Lord wants this message delivered now." (Ibid., p. 3.) He discussed at least nineteen facets of pride that I thought, as I looked at them, had destructive implications for marriages and family life. I can touch only briefly on them here but would invite you to consider in greater detail these elements of pride and their impact on marriage and family relations.

1. *Selfishness and pride lead to competitiveness.* The spirit of competition is an especially deadly virus in marriage because it prevents a couple from freely exchanging ideas and feelings with each other. Such discussions, they feel, might cause them to give up power in the relationship. Their goal of exaltation becomes an impossible feat if they compete rather than cooperate.

Sometimes patriarchal leadership is misconstrued and exercised inappropriately by husbands, almost as if they were competing with their family members. I've known men who felt that if their wives or children held opinions that differed with theirs, they were not honoring his priesthood. What a sad distortion of the majesty and beauty of priesthood authority! Apparently some men feel that their position in the family is an authorization to be tyrannical, though they would not interpret their behavior as such.

In the workplace, men and women are pitted against each other in ways that minimize appreciation for the gifts and talents of each sex. Sexual harassment is a problem that may be rooted in gender competition. Much of the radical feminist movement centers in some women's attempts to outcompete men in the marketplace for jobs, position, status, and salary. "Men bashing" has become fashionable in many circles, while uncomplimentary remarks are hurled at the feminine side. The clear and obvious danger here is the development of hatred for the opposite sex—a position diametrically opposed to gospel principles.

2. *Pride causes us to seek the adoration and approval of the world.* This element of pride, as it relates to marriage, causes priorities to be "out of whack." Proverbs 23:7 states, "As he thinketh in his heart, so is he." When priorities are centered on worldly approval and position, marriage and family suffer.

"I wish I were number one in my husband's life," Mary Jane told me. "Everything and everybody else comes before me. We hardly see him, and our children could use a lot more father than what they are getting. Why can't he see that we need him at home?"

It is as the Lord said: "No man can serve two masters: for either he will hate the one, and love the other; or else he will hold to the one, and despise the other. Ye cannot serve God and mammon." (Matthew 6:24.) If we seek to acquire more things in order to gain supposed status, we work longer and longer hours while families see less and less of us. When both parents leave the home to seek more of the world's goods, the children naturally suffer—though ironically most parents would argue that they are "doing all of this for the children." The most important priorities of men and women must be each other and their children.

3. *Pride is rarely admitted in ourselves but readily observed in others.* In troubled marriages, both individuals often seem blind to the fact that they may be the main contributors to the very problems of which they complain. Though it may be easier for a third party to identify and label their problems, only they can resolve them.

I recall James and Cathy, who criticized each other in front of me for some time before I interjected, "Jim, I understand how you feel about all of this, but if we are going to turn this around, what could *you* personally do to improve your marriage?" I thought it was a reasonable question, but the look on his face suggested I had stumped him. He had no idea that he might be frustrating his wife. He stammered, stuttered, and upon my insistence finally blurted out, "I suppose I could let her know that I am going to the club after work and that I might be a little later than usual." To him, not informing his wife that he might be late was the worst thing he was doing to hurt their marital relationship. (Incidentally, it was not even one of the things Cathy had mentioned in her list!)

When I asked Cathy what she could do to change the situation, it seemed to also catch her off guard. She couldn't think of *any* changes she should make. She was shocked that I could not see that she was wonderful and that it was her husband who was the obvious culprit; she thought anybody trained in family relations would see that. Yet I could see countless changes both of them could make to help the marriage work. Each finally agreed to meet some demands—*if* the partner was willing to do the same in return. I felt like a labor-relations negotiator.

Carlfred Broderick has perceptively commented on this blindness:

> After weeks, or even months and years of frustration, the conclusion most people come to is that the problem lies in the character deficiencies of their spouses. If only their partners weren't so lazy or selfish or uncaring or stupid or immature or oversexed or frigid or under the evil influence of their mothers . . . then perhaps there might be hope. Others come to the less popular but still common conclusion that the deficiencies lie in themselves—that they are the ones who are unforgivably crazy, unattractive or dumb. (*Couples* [New York: Simon and Schuster, 1987], p. 16.)

I suppose that to retain our mental health, we automatically defend what is reality to us. If we did not have some confidence in our perceptions, our mental health would probably crumble from internal dissonance. It is important to our state of mind that we can rely on our discernment, but that does not mean our view is the only correct one or that it is even accurate. Humility, the opposite of pride, includes the ability to look inward and take responsibility for one's contribution to the problem and then to change responses in order to better the relationship.

4. *Sins of pride lead to faultfinding, gossiping, backbiting, murmuring, living beyond one's means, envying, coveting, withholding gratitude and praise that might lift another, refusal to forgive, and jealousy.* These elements of pride are all too common in troubled marriages. Money problems, for example, usually stem from living beyond a couple's means, coveting what others have, or trying to "keep up with the Joneses." Many a marriage has been shipwrecked on the shoals of poor money management, arising from the desire not only to have but also to have more than anyone else, or to boost low self-esteem by accumulating possessions.

"Withholding gratitude and praise" may be among the most serious sins in the above list. This hinders change in too many marriages. Spouses should be profuse but sincere in their appreciation and compliments to each other and to other family members.

After discussing it over with his wife, Roberta, and me, Steve decided he was going to be a better leader in his home by calling the family together every night to read a chapter of scripture and have family prayer, something Roberta had wanted all her life. Steve performed this faithfully for a few days, and Roberta was pleased, though she hesitated to compliment him on his new behavior. She apparently justified her nonreinforcement of his actions with this rationale: "He is only doing this because the counselor talked him into it. Steve has tried to change before. It lasts about a week, and then it stops. I already know the outcome. If he goes another week, I'll really be surprised."

With that attitude, she said nothing to him in the way of thanks, though she had claimed this pattern of gathering the family together was very important to her. In the meantime, Steve wondered if he was pleasing her, if he was "doing it right," for she didn't seem to be any happier. He became discouraged. After two weeks, he exploded, "I told you that was not the real problem in our marriage. I've done my best, and it hasn't made any difference to you at all!" All of which, of course, confirmed Roberta's theory that Steve's change would last a short time and then stop. She was "right," after all, and perhaps she took more satisfaction in being right than in noticing any change on Steve's part. If she had acknowledged Steve's efforts, expressed her pleasure at the new turn of events, and noted aloud that it was making a difference in the spirit in their home, it could have made a world of difference. It would have helped him to know that he was meeting her expectations, and I have no doubts that he would have continued the family scripture study. But she would never know. Even if the reading was not quite the way she thought it should go, Steve needed her encouragement, not her criticism and withholding of appreciation.

Fortunately, there was a happy ending to this story after Roberta learned the importance of "shaping." Shaping is the process of reinforcing desired behavior in others. When your spouse or family members approximate your ideal, you simply let them know how pleased you are with their performance.

It is too bad we are the world's experts on the faults of our partners when we ought to be their cheerleaders. We ought to be thankful for the wonderful gifts and talents each brings to the marriage. No one is perfect, of course, but we can be grateful for the contributions our spouses and children make to our lives and express that love and appreciation both verbally and nonverbally. When we acknowledge others' efforts, they feel good about themselves and will usually continue the behavior that is complimented and recognized.

5. *Pride leads to selfishness.* We have already discussed President Kimball's identification of selfishness as the leading factor in divorce. It can sneak in and burrow itself almost unseen into our souls. In describing how selfishness destroys marriage, President Kimball said:

> Sometimes the ceaseless pinpricking of an unhappy, discontented, and selfish spouse can finally add up to serious physical violence. Sometimes people are goaded to the point where they erringly feel justified in doing the things which are so wrong. Nothing, of course, justifies sin.
>
> Sometimes a wife or a husband feels neglected, mistreated, and ignored until he or she wrongly feels justified in adding to the errors.

Then he suggested this remedy:

> If each spouse submits to frequent self-analysis and measures his own imperfections by the yardstick of perfection and the Golden

Rule, and if each spouse sets about to correct self in every devia-
tion found by such analysis rather than to set about to correct the
deviations in the other party, then transformation comes and happiness is the result. There are many pharisaic people who marry
who should memorize the parable of the Savior in Luke—people
who prate their own virtues and pile up their own qualities of
goodness and put them on the scales against the weaknesses of
the spouse. They say, "I fast twice a week; I give tithes of all I possess" (see Luke 18:12).

For every friction, there is a cause; and whenever there is unhappiness, each should search self to find the cause or at least
that portion of the cause which originated in that self.

. . . The marriage can be a successful one so long as selfishness does not enter in. Troubles and problems will draw parents
together into unbreakable unions if there is total unselfishness
there. . . .

The marriage that is based upon selfishness is almost certain
to fail. ("Marriage and Divorce," in *1976 Devotional Speeches of the
Year* [Provo, Utah: Brigham Young University Press, 1977], pp.
148–49.)

As President Kimball said, nothing, of course, justifies sin.
Mormon explained that the Nephite nation fell because of
pride: "Behold, the pride of this nation . . . hath proven their
destruction" (Moroni 8:27). Could it not be said of a couple,
"Behold, the pride of [these two] hath proven their destruction"? Indicators of pride include displays of temper, unrighteous judgments, growling at traffic lights or other drivers, anger
at Little League coaches or players, fits of anger over inanimate
objects, criticism of spouse and children, throwing the wrench
across the garage, and the like.

Most of us are humble in the initial stages of marriage, for
we are new to our marital roles. At that point in time we don't
have all the answers—yet. The honeymoon stage is upon us for
a while. Things seem perfect as we explore our relationship and
set up housekeeping with our wedding gifts in tow. We furnish
our apartment in early Deseret Industries or Salvation Army
style. We are willing to learn from each other at that point in
our lives. How quickly that seems to disappear as we become
more familiar with each other's weaknesses and acquire a few of
this world's goods!

It takes two partners to maintain a strong marriage and two to destroy it. Of course, one partner can, through serious misconduct and sin, be responsible for much of the damage, but even then, can there be a completely innocent party? I've never seen anyone, at least, willing to take all the blame. Everyone seems capable of justifying their actions and finding socially acceptable ways of explaining their behavior, whether or not such explanations are accurate.

6. *Pride leads to secret combinations.* Though this element of pride as well as the description of secret combinations in the scriptures may have little or no direct relation to a discussion of marriage, the word *secret* does suggest an important issue that is worth mentioning here. That issue is secret behaviors that create distance between two spouses. I often hear husbands say, "I don't tell my wife everything about our finances, because she would not approve of some of my investments." Keeping secrets from one another, unfortunately, is all too common in marriage. Frequently wives or husbands collude with children to hide information from spouses, fearful that the husband or wife will not approve or that discipline will be too harsh; such collusion may result from one spouse's desire to be protective. But hoping that a spouse does not find out about a decision can have a major impact on marital happiness. There is danger in one spouse's making decisions that drastically affect the fate of both partners.

7. *Pride leads to contention—arguments, fights, unrighteous dominion, generation gaps, divorces, spouse abuse, riots, and disturbances of all kinds.* Herein lies a whole host of afflictions that spring from pride. Contention and anger are the great destroyers of family relations. We suffer two ways when we display a temper. One is that we lose the Spirit of the Lord, for the Holy Ghost is very sensitive to how we treat others, especially those of our own household. And second, other people do not want to be near us. Temperamental people are not popular people. We've all seen "old grouches." Without the Spirit of the Lord to soften and humble us, we easily slip into condemning and judging others unrighteously, and we contend with family members over trivial issues. Who likes to be around someone who is argumentative and angry? "I would that ye should remember, and always retain in remembrance, the greatness of God, and your

own nothingness," King Benjamin warned his people and, by extension, all of us. In this same address he also said: "And ye will not have a mind to injure one another, but live peaceably. . . . And ye will not suffer your children . . . that they transgress the laws of God, and fight and quarrel one with another, and serve the devil, who is the master of sin." (Mosiah 4:11, 13–14.)

We hear so much about abuse these days—of wives, of children, and occasionally of husbands. Nothing causes more damage in marriage and family relations than uncontrolled anger that leads to verbal or physical assaults. Bruised feelings damaged by senseless temper tantrums may never recover. How immature we are to let pride cause us to harm the very ones we invited to be a part of our eternal family! How silly we are to think we can be temperamental and still attain the celestial kingdom! How shortsighted we become when we lose our long-range perspective!

8. *Pride leads to our using the social approval of others to determine our worth and value.* For the Nephites, setting their hearts on riches was a major contributor to their downfall. Similarly, valuing material things or assets more than we value individuals sooner or later leads to heartbreak. Parents who vent their anger on children who have dropped their peanut butter sandwich or drink on the car seat have forgotten that they too were young once. Car seats can be cleaned, but young minds can be permanently damaged by cumulative ridicule.

Speaking of us and our time, Moroni lamented: "Why do ye adorn yourselves with that which hath no life, and yet suffer the hungry, and the needy, and the naked, and the sick and the afflicted to pass by you, and notice them not?" (Mormon 8:39.) We do not seek riches to bless others but rather to heap upon ourselves more than others possess. (Athletes comparing the size of their contracts with those of other athletes comes to mind.) The Book of Mormon describes the "great pride which had gotten into the hearts of the people; and it was because of their exceedingly great riches and their prosperity in the land; and it did grow upon them from day to day" (Helaman 3:36). Then it explains how this attitude led to the destruction of the people:

> Now this great loss of the Nephites, and the great slaughter which was among them, would not have happened had it not

been for their wickedness and their abomination which was
among them. . . .

And it was because of the pride of their hearts, because of
their exceeding riches, yea, it was because of their oppression to
the poor, withholding their food from the hungry, withholding
their clothing from the naked, and smiting their humble brethren
upon the cheek, making a mock of that which was sacred, denying
the spirit of prophecy and of revelation, murdering, plundering,
lying, stealing, committing adultery, rising up in great con-
tentions, . . .

And because of this their great wickedness, and their boast-
ings in their own strength, they were left in their own strength;
therefore they did not prosper, but were afflicted and smitten . . .
until they had lost possession of almost all their lands. (Helaman
4:11–13.)

Could it be that we have so many more material possessions
than the Nephites did that our level of pride, selfishness, and
arrogance dwarfs theirs? Without BMWs, TVs, VCRs, radial
tires, wristwatches, dishwashers, central air and heat, wrinkle-
free clothing, and medical cures, they still managed to become
prideful. We have been inundated with many more conveniences and luxuries conducive to prideful feelings than they
were. Yet, pride destroyed the Nephites. And our prophets are
describing us as having similar tendencies. Are we so money
conscious, materially oriented, and insecure that we are headed
down the same Nephite path?

9. *Pride limits and stops progression; we become no longer teach-
able.* Marriage involves a profound commitment to teach and
learn from each other. Most of us come to marriage with little
solid experience except of our own family background. Consequently, marriage requires us to gently teach family members
and, in turn, to humbly desire to learn from each one of them.
Quality family relations require an appreciation for the contribution of each family member. We must protect the self-esteem
of our spouse and children. Who else would or could do it as
well? May I ask you: What kind of teacher and student are you
in your own home? How able are you to learn from your spouse
or children?

Sometimes a wife will tell me, "I have been trying for twenty
years to get my husband to . . . ," and she will outline a particular

thing she wishes he would do. I often think to myself, *If you have been trying for twenty years to get your husband to start or stop a particular behavior, you must not be a very good teacher!* Of course, I would not say that to her. But if that is *not* true, then the only other possibility as I see it is that her husband's pride prevents him from learning from her.

I remember an occasion when a teacher, after a long class period on teaching techniques, brought out a cake to share with the students as a refreshment break. After passing out napkins to everyone, he began to distribute the cake by tearing a chunk with his bare hand and placing it on each student's napkin as he passed down the row. Everyone was dumbfounded. Nobody was eating. Why not? There was nothing wrong with the cake. But it was not a very pleasant way to eat, regardless of the quality of the confection! After the teacher explained that we may serve lessons to our students in unattractive ways, out came the china, cloth napkins, and silverware, and the group enjoyed a pleasant respite.

The lesson was clear. Many people use terrible teaching methods. In marriages and families these can include nagging, griping, silence, screaming, or a spouse's withholding sex for a period of time. These *are* teaching techniques, no question about it, but they are not very effective if we want our students to function cheerfully and willingly. Rather, these techniques usually create bitterness and anger.

In the home, effective teaching works hand in hand with humble learning. How willing are you to learn when your spouse is the instructor? Can you name one thing you have learned from him or her recently? Even more difficult, are you willing to learn from your children?

10. *Pride causes us to ignore God and the needs of others.* We live in a day of glorifying the "self." We are preoccupied with satisfying our own needs rather than those of others. Pride has no need for God or any higher power that wants us to control or restrict our appetites. Instead of "Thy will be done," the refrain is "I will do it my way." Inevitably, our marriage and family suffer.

11. *Pride separates us by rank according to our riches and education.* It seems that as we obtain a little cache of this world's goods, we want more. Soon, we want to distance ourselves from

others who are not in our same class, and we begin to feel that others are inferior. We not only want to fly first class but also want to do it at others' expense.

The Nephite society was frequently divided because of material possessions and educational level (see 3 Nephi 6:12). Focusing on position and status rather than service negates our value in the kingdom. Feelings of superiority are un-Christlike. Are we not all sons and daughters of the same Heavenly Father? We are partners in carrying out God's work. We are equal before him and dependent on each other. I have known several men like the one who acquired a Ph.D. that was financed mostly by a wife who worked while also caring for their children. Later he left her, complaining they "had nothing in common anymore." Apparently his education and intellect made him independent of the very one who had been his champion and sacrificed for his success. "To be learned is good," said Jacob, "if [we] hearken unto the counsels of God" (2 Nephi 9:29).

12. *Pride causes our feelings for Christ to fade, resulting in a loss of the Spirit.* Without Christ, we are nothing. There would be no resurrection to allow eternal marriage, no priesthood power to seal couples in matrimony, and absolutely no way to overcome sin, which prevents exaltation. Without Christ, mortality would be a dead end.

13. *Pride makes it impossible to develop unity.* The proud lose the spirit of cooperation and oneness. Spouses' different priorities threaten unity. Cooperation is essential if we are to bring our family together in harmony, for little can be accomplished if we are not united in our goals. "If ye are not one ye are not mine" (D&C 38:27). Husbands and wives suffering from this symptom will often find their children pitting one parent against the other in destructive ways.

14. *Pride prevents confessing and forsaking sins, for there is no recognition of a need to change behavior.* "What is there to change?" asks one who is proud. "What is wrong with the way I am doing it? If you were in my shoes, you would see that I am doing it the very best way."

Arrogance brings no desire to repent or change for the better. Such people think they came from the "true family" and have no need to change for the sake of others. Instead, they feel others need to bow to their expectations.

A difficult step in repentance is to recognize our sins and our obvious need to apologize and correct our behavior. Unless we can assume responsibility for our errors, how can we build eternal relationships with others?

"I kept telling my wife how much she reminded me of her mother," Garth told me. "One day, in front of her sister and my brother-in-law, I made one of those dumb comments. As soon as I said it, I felt the Spirit of the Lord leave me. I looked at my wife, whom I could tell I had injured. She turned to her sister and said, 'Garth thinks I am just like our mom.'

"I struggled to get the Spirit back by discounting the whole event. I thought that by ignoring it, it would go away. I kept saying to myself, *I was just kidding*. But it didn't help. I tried telling myself, *Well, I was just having a little fun with her. She knows that I wasn't serious*. To no avail. I tried another: *Well, she does remind me of her mother, and I was just being honest about it and pointing it out to her*. That only made things worse.

"Finally—and it was into the next day now—I told her that I was sorry I had made such comments, that I knew better and I would stop them. My wife looked at me and said, 'Well, I guess I can't help it. I know I'm like her.'

"I said, 'No, that isn't the issue at all. You know that I love you and your mom, and I was out of order in my teasing.' We hugged, and for the first time in two days I felt a return of the Spirit of the Lord. I learned a great lesson."

15. *Pride prevents forgiveness of others.* The proud condemn, criticize, and bear grudges. Forgiveness requires a softened heart, the spirit of love, and the application of the Golden Rule. Putting ourselves in the shoes of another—our companion and little ones—as well as remembering our own youthful mistakes and our simple but wrong logic in many instances can help smooth bumped and bruised egos.

Many of us will not allow our partner or children to repent and change, either. We continue to bring up past experiences or statements as if they were still relevant. The Lord's willingness to forgive us is commensurate with our willingness to forgive others. The proud husband or wife cannot bring himself or herself to pardon others.

16. *Pride keeps young men, young women, and couples from serving missions.* With only one-third of our young men going on

missions, it is obvious that too many of our young people are caught in the pride trap. Sharing time and talents for two years or eighteen months does require sacrifice of personal time and means. The selfish and proud cannot do it. For some, there are too many distractions, it seems, to take time out to serve the Lord. If the Lord has asked every young man in the Church to serve a mission, where are they all? Why do so many not go? Because they can't see themselves giving up trucks, stereos, hairstyles, immorality, education, or sin to serve God. But, oh, what they miss out on! Missions convert missionaries. Young men and women gain insights and testimony that are worth far more than any gain that could be accrued by their staying home. The fact that two-thirds of our young men are refusing missionary service is, to put it bluntly, a shame and a sad commentary on the extent to which pride has gripped the hearts of our youth in a day of ease and prosperity.

17. *Pride prevents yielding one's heart to God.* Giving of oneself to do the Lord's bidding and inviting all people to come to Jesus Christ should be our main objectives. He who would save his life must first lose it. Doing "what thou would have me do" is not the sentiment of those whose hearts are filled with pride.

"Disobedience is essentially a prideful power struggle against someone in authority over us," said President Benson. "It can be a parent, a priesthood leader, a teacher, or ultimately God. A proud person hates the fact that someone is above him. He thinks this lowers his position." (In Conference Report, April 1989, p. 5.) A person's yielding so that God can use him or her to carry out his great latter-day work requires the opposites of pride—humility, meekness, submissiveness. President Benson declared: "God will have a humble people. Either we can choose to be humble or we can be compelled to be humble. Alma said, 'Blessed are they who humble themselves without being compelled to be humble' (Alma 32:16). Let us choose to be humble." (Ibid., p. 6.)

18. *Pride prevented continuation of the law of consecration among the Nephites.* Pride does not allow free-will offerings of earnings, property, or time. We cannot establish Zion without a willingness to live the law of consecration. Its implementation failed in Missouri during the early days of the restored Church

in part because the Saints could not live the principle for an extended period without jealousy and envy destroying their efforts.

The question for us today is: Would we succeed any better than the early Saints in living this principle this time around? Certainly one reason for its failure in an earlier day was the inability of some members to detach themselves from their possessions. In this final dispensation this principle again will be established as it is embraced by those whose allegiance to God and his Zion is greater than their attraction to the things of this world.

The principles of the law of consecration are the same principles that strengthen marriages and families—a willingness to sacrifice one's time, talent, and resources to bless those of our own household, as well as those in the ward and the community.

19. *Pride is the great "stumbling block" to Zion.* Zion is defined as "the pure in heart," signifying individuals who love God and their fellowmen. The economic order of Zion will not be established again until people are willing to let go of their strong attachments to personal possessions and can share with others so that all may benefit.

"They have not learned to be obedient to the things which I required at their hands," the Lord explained of the early Saints and their inability to build Zion, "but are full of all manner of evil, and do not impart of their substance, as becometh saints, to the poor and afflicted among them; and are not united according to the union required by the law of the celestial kingdom; and Zion cannot be built up unless it is by the principles of the law of the celestial kingdom; otherwise I cannot receive her unto myself" (D&C 105:3–5).

Pride is the great stumbling block not only to Zion but also to a great marriage, a stumbling block that must be removed first from individual hearts, then families, then communities, and finally the world. Zion cannot be established except on principles of personal sacrifice and a willingness to care for others as much as we care for ourselves. To establish Zion requires willing hearts and minds—attributes contrary to pride. Our homes are the seedbeds for rearing a Zion people.

Summary

The Book of Mormon message reminds us that when people have political freedom, economic prosperity, leisure time, and material possessions, inevitably pride, selfishness, and the desire for class systems and status begin to grow in their hearts. Pride arises from, as President Benson pointed out, "enmity toward God and enmity toward our fellowmen" (in Conference Report, April 1989, p. 3); it views others as competitors in the race to acquire worldly goods. God commands us to give freely, but pride does not yield easily. Pride and its close relative selfishness are the great stumbling blocks to happy marriages and the establishment of Zion in the latter days.

CHAPTER NINE

Keys to Success in Marriage Relationships

Marital growth, as I conceive it," writes Carl-fred Broderick, "comes from increasing the amount of personal support each partner feels from the other, and from decreasing the number of put-downs and disappointments received." He continues, as stated in the previous chapter, "The conclusion most people come to is that the problem lies in the character deficiencies of their spouses." (*Couples* [New York: Simon and Schuster, 1987], pp. 15–16.)

These two issues—the lack of personal support, and focus-ing on the character deficiencies of a spouse or child—are two serious mistakes (sins, really) that undo marriages and handi-cap the building of strong families. Derogatory statements de-stroy self-worth, while blame and accusations create defensive-ness and prevent change and healing.

Those with healthy marriages focus on their partners' strengths and are quick to compliment them on what they do well. Most of us are aware of our weaknesses without constant reminders. Those who emphasize the defects of others often use those inadequacies as excuses for their own less-than-celestial behavior, and are, in their own right, contributing to family contention. An old cliché says, "Every husband has grounds for a divorce; every wife has grounds for a divorce," meaning that if any of us took the time to concentrate on the weaknesses of our spouse, we could undoubtedly come up with a number of irritating habits or behaviors that we might interpret as grounds for incompatibility. In fact, if we thought about them very long, we might get quite worked up about them. But most of us have sense enough to realize that eighty-five to ninety-five percent of our relationship works well and that it would be foolish to keep harping on trivial issues that, in all likelihood, will not change anyway. Carol might be less of a housekeeper than Charles would like her to be, but that is not a sufficient reason to break up the marriage. There are better ways to resolve this irritation. Carol might not like the sexual technique her husband uses in their lovemaking, but that is not sufficient reason to have an affair, seek a divorce, or complain to the bishop. Better solutions are available.

When any marital difference between spouses becomes all-consuming, the entire relationship may be poisoned. Changing a spouse's behavior, for example, is a two-edged sword. If it is something really irritating, usually a calm discussion is in order as to why a behavior change might improve the marriage. After all, we have agency, and most of us are free to do things differently if we think it might improve our marital happiness. Christlike people are anxious to learn and to improve. Or, it might be better to accept the uniqueness of a spouse than to try to refit him or her into your shoes. Putting your prescription glasses on another may not help that person's vision at all! Perhaps more important, ask yourself why this particular change seems so crucial anyway.

Perhaps your spouse uses words of which he or she is unaware. For example, your spouse may frequently say "you know" in casual conversation, or, if he or she is from the Intermountain West, may have grown up saying "she come" rather than "came," or "I seen" rather than "I saw." A gentle discussion with a spouse, with a return promise to "tell me when I err," ought to suffice. If corrections only stir resentment, it may not be worth the effort. Much depends on the attitude of the spouse. Constant harping on faults is not conducive to the Spirit of the Lord, nor is it pleasant to be around someone who is watching every word we say. Partners may move from "you know" to "you've always criticized me" rather easily. Most of us do not see eye-to-eye with our spouses on everything but are sufficiently mature to appreciate how insignificant such irritations are compared with the good our spouses do. Besides, if we are mature, we know by now that "we ain't so hot either, baby." We all could benefit from reviewing occasionally the Savior's teachings on the mote and beam (see Matthew 7:3–5).

Increasing Personal Support

Every human being has two major needs—physical and emotional, or spiritual. All human beings require the essentials—air, water, food, clothing—to sustain physical life. But we also need emotional and spiritual sustenance. This life support usually comes in the form of positive information or feedback from important others in our lives—most notably, family members. If these people love us and express their love frequently and genuinely, our self-worth is enhanced. On the other hand, if we live with constant criticism we can be devastated or feel nervous about whatever we say and do. We feel we are "walking on eggshells."

We all need to feel loved, valued, and cherished, not just as receivers but also as contributors. These processes confirm in our minds and hearts that we are "okay," that we are acceptable and normal. This need for approval is powerful and constitutes an important element of every human being's emotional makeup. When positive feedback is given and received, emotional bonds are established and strengthened between individuals, and behavior is reinforced.

I call these positives *validation*—feedback that affirms our worth and value. Such validation may be verbal, such as, "I don't know what I would do without you" or "I love being married to you." Nonverbal expressions might include a gentle touch or squeeze of the hand, an embrace, and sexual intimacy. Validation directly conveys appreciation, love, and respect. The more specific the compliment, the more valuable and strengthening it is to the relationship. "One reason I love you is that you always are happy to see me come home, stop what you are doing, and greet me, and I like that," is more helpful than "I love you." In marriage, two partners who provide fairly constant and genuinely positive feedback to each other will rate their marriage high on the satisfaction scale. Reciprocal and ongoing validation contributes to our emotional health and stability. Criticism very quickly destroys incentive and love.

Risk-Trust Dimensions

Another way to view this concept of feedback in family relationships is to observe what happens when one person risks his or her own personal ideas or feelings with another. I use the word *risk* because the message sender is often apprehensive as to how the receiver will respond to the message. When a message is received, there is always a response by the other party. Even when a husband merely continues to watch the ball game—with no outward indication that he has heard the message—he is responding! A person's willingness to risk personal feelings and ideas with someone else is based largely on the quality of previous exchanges with that person. Each relationship seems to develop a personality of its own.

Negative Risking

When an individual discloses personal ideas, opinions, or values with another and receives a negative response (sarcasm, put-down, interruption, sermon, judgment, and so on), the desire to continue to risk decreases dramatically. Consider the following model:

$$\textit{risk} \longrightarrow \begin{array}{c} \textit{negative} \\ \textit{response} \end{array} \longrightarrow \textit{stop risk}$$

Suppose that Jan is frustrated with her seven-year-old son, Randy, and approaches her husband, Richard, for help. Richard is watching a football game on TV. Jan says, "Rich, I need your help with Randy." The urgency in her voice indicates that he is needed now, and Jan expects Rich to respond immediately. If Rich does not come but is instead irritated that she has interrupted his ball-game watching, what negative response could he send his wife? Perhaps "Not now, I'm busy," or "Can't you handle it?" or "You pick the darnedest times to need my help." Or, he might even do nothing but continue to watch the game. There are many possible negative responses. If this pattern were common in Jan and Rich's marriage—if he consistently ignores or "burns" her with negative responses when she wants to engage him—what would you predict their relationship would develop into? Obviously Jan would be frustrated, would probably risk less, would lose confidence in her ability to gain her husband's assistance, and would undoubtedly lose respect for him because he seems unwilling to assume his parental duties. Ball games are more important to him than she or Randy is, as she sees it. She might stop asking for his help, knowing that he won't respond, and will probably become irritated. Furthermore, she might withdraw from Rich, and her resentment could show up somewhere else in the relationship. If it's not in the bedroom, it may be when Rich needs her help on a matter. Reciprocity is an important principle in human relationships.

This is not an uncommon pattern between husbands and wives and between parents and their children. Imagine a child approaching his father and asking if he can go with his friends to a party. The father, who does not like his son's friends, looks for an excuse and says, "You haven't cleaned up that mess in the garage or taken care of the pile of junk in the backyard. Now, get those things taken care of before you ask to go anywhere." If a pattern develops between the father and son in which the father predictably will try to prevent his son from being with his friends, what do you predict will happen to their relationship? There are several possibilities. For example, the son may not ask for his father's permission anymore, may sneak around to avoid confrontation with his father, or may be obedient to his father's request but be inwardly resentful. Most of us try to avoid pain or punishment.

This pattern of

$$\text{risk} \longrightarrow \begin{array}{c} \textit{negative} \\ \textit{response} \end{array} \longrightarrow \text{risk less}$$

destroys communication in marriages and families. As less and less risk occurs, stress and strain develop because we become quite superficial and our relationships don't grow in closeness or strength. When this pattern develops, it is critical that people like Rich and Jan or Rich and his son realize that theirs is a problem that needs attention. They need to "meta-communicate," that is, to talk together about how they talk together, as well as about what they are thinking and feeling regarding the way issues and problems are being resolved. Jan and Rich need to discuss the episode concerning Randy and the ball game when they are not upset or emotional, and they need to try to understand what happened and how they might handle it differently next time. Rich, if he were Christlike, would support Jan, apologize, and resolve that he will help next time. And Jan might be wise to wait until a commercial before making her request, then ask how the game is going, and be more explicit about the emergency with Randy.

The most desirable outcome is for each spouse to be responsive to the other's requests. If a ball game is more important to Rich than a pressing family situation, he needs to review his priorities. In the case of a father-son relationship, children do not usually initiate a time to talk about real-life situations that need to be reviewed together. Most likely, parents will need to initiate visits with their children about issues that arise and need discussion. Meta-communication is an excellent way to work out an acceptable compromise in most situations.

Positive Risking—the Development of Love

Suppose that when we disclose personal feelings or thoughts with another, the person's response to our ideas is positive. We then have this model:

risk ⟶ *positive response* ⟶ *willingness to risk again*

When we share personal ideas, opinions, values, and feelings with another, a rapport begins to develop between us because it meets our individual need to communicate with other human beings. We especially desire this type of communication with a member of the opposite sex, and we believe that marriage will be the ultimate setting in which to share mentally, emotionally, spiritually, and physically. We anticipate being able to risk and reveal ideas and thoughts with a spouse that we do not share with anyone else. It is through such sharing and validating that we build strong marital bonds.

In a very real sense, this process of risking is how people "fall in love." First dates, for example, are usually superficial, but as we begin to date someone with whom we can safely exchange deeper thoughts and feelings, we begin to develop a friendship and enjoy being together. We value our associations with individuals with whom we can relax and be ourselves. By risking core beliefs, philosophies, and feelings with another, we lay a foundation for trust to grow. As our sharing continues, an emotional attachment develops because we realize that we can share without ridicule, and that we can be genuine, with no facades, no relationship games or power plays or struggles with which to contend. We simply share our heart and soul with another human being. It is an awesome experience to peer into the soul of another, to probe the depths of their feelings. We come to appreciate that we are unique beings, sons and daughters of God, with similar feelings and goals. It gives meaning to our own existence when we grasp the very essence of what makes others tick, especially our own spouse and children. We walk on holy ground on such occasions, and it is incumbent that we treat our information reverently as these relationships become sacred and profound. Too, we gain confidence in our ideas when we find others accept them and have similar ideas as well. Thus, each validates the worth and value of the other. Our need for expressing our core selves is fulfilled through such dialogues in our intimate settings, and strong bonds of love are then built.

Rejection Destroys Relationships

Personal rejection, on the other hand, leaves a person vulnerable to hurt and embarrassment. When I asked Susan why she did not greet her husband, Jon, with a hug and a kiss when he came home from work, she replied, "He would push me away or wonder what I did to the car." The probability of personal rejection was too painful for her to even attempt greeting him warmly. Obviously there had been a history of negative experiences. Though she agreed with me that greeting in this way was a good idea "for other couples," she would not allow herself to be hurt by her husband's rebuffs, and the relationship suffered.

Because validation is a sincere and positive conveyance of love, value, and acceptance, great marriages are characterized by an abundance of these messages. Husbands and wives with healthy relationships find it easy to validate each other, thus building and strengthening their bonds of love and dependence. In contrast, couples with a history of anger and frustration find validation difficult, if not seemingly impossible. Positive communication between two people is the lifeblood of any close relationship, and this is especially true in marriage. In fact, without a fairly frequent dose of validation most of us find life discouraging or depressing, to say the least. Unchecked, unresolved rejection can lead to anger, hostility, violent retaliation, and eventual divorce. Rather than feel rejected, every soul needs to know that he or she is loved, appreciated, and valued, and that he or she plays an important role in the marriage and family.

Application

Let's make sure we can apply this information to our marriages.

Husbands: How does your wife receive love and appreciation for the contribution she is making as a mother, homemaker, confidante, and lover? The answer is that she receives it from you and the children, who verbally and nonverbally express to her your love and appreciation for her contribution to your lives as a wife or mother.

Wives: How does your husband receive esteem, love, and positive strokes for his contribution as your husband and the father of your children? He receives it from you and the children as you express both verbally and nonverbally your love and appreciation to him.

Parents: How do your children develop feelings of confidence, competence, and self-worth that enable them to deal with their challenges? They develop these feelings when you value them and communicate that worth to them frequently and genuinely. Their confidence in themselves and in their abilities will blossom as you verbally and nonverbally frequently convey your love.

How does the bishop, elders quorum leader, Relief Society president, company president, businessperson, dogcatcher—anyone—have these basic needs fulfilled? These needs to feel loved, appreciated, and valued are filled by the important people in their lives too.

Now the mystery! If most of us understand this principle, why is it so hard to express our love to those around us? Why do we wait until the viewing and funeral to express our appreciation for the departed? Why can't we be more expressive of our love and gratitude while friends and family members are still living and breathing? We could do so much to lighten the load for so many through simple, genuine expressions of respect and appreciation. Counselors see too many people who are love-starved and crying out for some morsel of validation.

On the other hand, why do we use negative, critical behavior in an effort to motivate each other when it is clear that we ourselves function better when we receive positive feedback? Why are we so slow to apply these principles? Yes, there needs to be discipline and firmness with children; we don't say yes to everything they want. But most people who need correction or redirection are already aware that they have made a mistake or that they are exceeding good sense. When we take delight in pointing out flaws, in extracting "payment in full," we lose friends and devastate family members. And we may be wrong; we may misjudge intent. Perhaps they did their best and made a sincere, genuine miscalculation. Don't we all? Where is compassion? Charity? Certainly there are times when we must "reprove betimes with sharpness, when moved upon by the Holy Ghost." When that is necessary, the Lord tells us that we would be wise to show forth "afterwards an increase of love toward him whom thou hast reproved, lest he esteem thee to be his enemy." (See D&C 121:43–44.) We often forget that part!

Remember, our basic needs for love and esteem are met through positive interactions with others, where feelings of love and worth are exchanged easily and freely. And positive touching, including hugs and squeezes—contact comfort—adds an important complimentary dimension to practically any relationship.

The Value of Validation in Relationships

When couples do not share personal thoughts, opinions, and ideas with each other because they have been hurt or rejected in their previous or present relationships, this does not mean there is little or no communication between the two. We often assume people are not communicating with each other if they are not talking, and we presume that the solution to most marital problems is to *increase* the amount of verbal communication between the pair.

I recall a particular presidential debate one election year. It was obvious that the two candidates did not like each other. They interrupted each other and would not let the other finish a sentence (much like some marrieds). To counsel these two candidates to "communicate more with each other" would not solve their problem, would it? No one wants to continue talking with someone who belittles their ideas or interrupts them. So, too, in our family environment it is important that each member be able to comfortably and safely share ideas and feelings without being put down or made to feel foolish.

A student of mine related the following:

> Ever since I was old enough to remember, our family was constantly together! We took many vacations and enjoyed each other's company. My dad loves our family more than anything in this world. He is always trying to make us happy and help us get the most out of life. He is very understanding and a great listener. He's always concerned for our needs and helps us out all he can to solve our problems. My dad always wants what's best for us. He's a very special dad.
>
> My mom loves to be involved in what we are doing. She supports us 100 percent! . . . Mom really cares and is interested in us! She is never the "boring mom!" She is fun and crazy with all of us kids. She is a very loving and caring person. Maybe that's why I get so homesick when I am away from her. She always comforts me. Sometimes I tease her and tell her she's a nosy mom because she likes to hear about all I do in my day. What a special, loving mom!

Discipline and the enforcement of family rules are also ways of conveying love and caring. Permissiveness as a method to win the love of children usually backfires, more clearly resembles indulgence than love, and does not build relationships built on respect. Parental insecurity, a lack of decisiveness, or attempting to win children over by never saying no leads to ever-increasing demands on the children's part. They easily sense their parents' weaknesses and learn to manipulate and exploit them. There are times when kings and queens must rule in their kingdom; otherwise the subjects—children—are wont to. Firmness in sustaining good family rules coupled with warm, nurturant, loving interaction between parents and children is the most effective and responsible kind of parenting. This is one way children develop a conscience. Without discipline, children do not learn self-control. They do not develop the ability to hear that inner voice that tells them something is right or wrong. When someone says no, we have to rethink the issues as well as our options. It causes us to look at all sides of a problem.

"Melissa, do you love your husband?" I asked a woman who had been married several years.

Her response: "I don't know whether I really love him anymore or not. I don't seem to have anymore feelings for him." From her answer it was obvious that she and her husband had stopped validating each other and sharing their intimate feelings, for that is the way love is generated and strengthened. They both admitted that they were not sending affirming messages back and forth. The consequence of this pattern is superficiality and negativism. Communication between Melissa and Ted had deteriorated to the point that no love messages were being sent or received. At this stage, positive feelings and emotions decline, and the relationship dies rather quickly.

Contention and validation are mutually exclusive. It would be difficult, if not impossible, for Melissa, in the midst of their contention, to say to Ted: "I know we are fighting a lot, dear, but I want you to know that I love you with all my heart." It would probably be dishonest as well. And when validation ceases, emotional distancing cannot be far behind. Typically each spouse begins to gather evidence to prove that the other is the chief offender. In an attempt to safeguard their own egos, they shut down communication and withdraw from each other and the relationship. Hostility heightens, and it is even more difficult to be positive. Each becomes defensive, and they rehash old problems in an attempt to escape dealing with the present, most pressing ones. Sexual relations become less frequent or nonexistent. Soon feelings of love are blunted or snuffed out, and the relationship dies from a lack of positive nourishment. Superficiality rules the day as feelings of love for each other slip away.

Happily married couples, on the other hand, freely share their thoughts and emotions on a fairly consistent basis. They are generally positive, certainly respectful. Each spouse has learned to express love for the other in ways that routinely fulfill the other's basic needs for love and human contact.

I asked Joan and Arnie: "Why are you two so happy?" Arnie's response: "I don't know. We just like being together. Sometimes we'll stay up late just talking and laughing together." What they are saying is that they are comfortable sharing personal ideas and feelings without any fear of being made to feel inferior.

Repentance and Forgiveness in Marriage

As we notice love feelings fading, we need to wake up and realize what we are doing to each other. Now is the time to remember the purpose of marriage and to remind ourselves that we made sacred covenants with God and with each other. We must take responsibility for our part of the damage, realizing that it took both of us to get into our present situation. We are both to blame. Did you trip on that last statement? It is hard to believe that we are as much to blame as our partner, for what we have done seems so logical to us. But it could actually be that we are responsible for *most* of the problem! However, the important thing is not to ascribe blame percentages but to repent and make needed changes. We need to begin the repair process.

I have always been interested in the fact that before we marry, had anyone asked us if we expected any problems in marriage, we would have admitted that the possibility was certainly there, though we couldn't quite imagine anything serious arising. Logically we agreed that problems could occur and that sound minds and hearts would be needed at *some* time in our upcoming marriage. Well, now is that time! It is here! The time for maturity has arrived; we are about to see just how Christlike we really are. We are not just adults but Latter-day Saint adults in a committed, covenant, eternal marriage relationship. When we experience problems in our relationship we need to step back, look at our differences with our eternal perspective, not panic and not create any further emotional damage, take responsibility, and then repent for any wrongdoings. Christlike attributes must now come into play. An important first step is to have the humility to realize we may have both lost the Spirit of the Lord, and that we need to have it restored. We then can take responsibility for our part of the situation, correct it, and preserve our own integrity and that of our spouse or children. Genuine repentance usually entails a sincere apology, which is the initial phase of the repair process. (One of the best talks on taking responsibility is that of Elder F. Burton Howard in Conference Report, April 1991, pp. 13–16.)

It takes two people to make a marriage function well, and it takes two to repair any damage. Each one must be personally committed to do better, try harder, change offensive behavior, please the other, reaffirm mutual commitments, and seek each other's and the Lord's forgiveness. That is the only way I know of to have the Spirit return when it has left. The Spirit is extremely sensitive to how we treat each other. When we are angry and say or do things contrary to gospel standards, we disappoint Heavenly Father and his Spirit is withdrawn. That alone should quickly humble us as we realize what we have done by offending the Lord's Spirit.

Our agency allows us to choose our responses; we are not victims. We do not accept the basic stimulus-response model without modification. The Latter-day Saint model looks like this:

stimulus ———————▶ *agency* ———————▶ *response*

Our ability to choose our responses makes us different from animals. We do have the choice to use our agency to restore relationships.

Jesus is our best example. On the cross, though experiencing superhuman pain and suffering, he pleaded for forgiveness in behalf of his executors, the Roman soldiers. While his Jewish captors spit on, smote, and scourged Jesus during and after his "trial," he calmly suffered these abominations "because of his loving kindness and his long-suffering towards the children of men" (1 Nephi 19:9). Manifesting charity even to the end of his life, Jesus was in control of his emotions. As Jesus' disciples we must learn from his example to forgive those who hurt us. We also must quickly seek forgiveness when we have erred.

It is at home with our families where most of us can best come to know each other's strengths and weaknesses. Here we will no doubt have plenty of practice in developing celestial attributes. If we are going to live the gospel, we must take responsibility for our wrongful actions, apologize, and resolve differences "because of [our] loving kindness and [our] long-suffering towards [members of our household]." To retaliate when we take offense is to act more like the adversary, Lucifer. If the Savior is our Exemplar, we must become like him in every way. We must be calm under pressure, and the self-esteem of others must be preserved and enhanced. We must initiate reconciliation. To ignore the Atonement, break covenants, or attempt to cover our sins with rationalization means that we reject repentance as a means of resolving differences. Too often, in our pride we accuse others or rationalize our own bad behavior and example by pointing out the faults of others in an effort to deflect them away from our own weaknesses.

We Can Change Our Responses

Susan, a young mother of three who was struggling in her marriage, asked, "Wouldn't it be better for me to get a divorce so that my children do not have to put up with all the bickering and fighting going on in our home? I know it's not good for the children, and it tears them apart." Susan is not the first to ask this question. It has been a difficult one for me to answer. It is a two-edged sword. If I were to say, "No, you should not divorce," they would think I was condoning the damage being done to both the adults and children in that family. If I answer, "Yes, I think you should divorce," I would be suggesting a breakup of a marriage where two have made covenants with God, a serious decision that is not my place to make.

I found an answer to this problem from President Spencer W. Kimball, an answer that I am convinced is one the Savior would give. It cuts right to the heart of the matter. He said: "Almost like a broken record [I hear from] divorcees that it is better to have [the children] grow up in a single-parent home than a fighting home. The answer to that specious argument is: there need be no battling parents in fighting homes." (*The Teachings of Spencer W. Kimball,* ed. Edward L. Kimball [Salt Lake City: Bookcraft, 1982], p. 314.) There *is* another option besides that of attacking, feuding, and destroying each other and our children. It is to repent, change, and stop the damaging responses we have used in the past. We have agency and can choose. We do not have to retaliate. (Abuse and meanness of spirit in time, of course, may be grounds for a divorce in order to preserve the mental health, sanity, and safety of a spouse and/or children.)

This matter of repentance is where the solution to marital problems really lies. President Gordon B. Hinckley has said that the remedy "is not found in divorce. It is found in the gospel of the Son of God. . . . The remedy for most marriage stress is not in divorce. It is in repentance. It is not in separation. It is in simple integrity that leads a man to square up his shoulders and meet his obligations." (In Conference Report, April 1991, p. 97.)

That has been my observation. In working with families for many years, I have yet to hear a husband or wife, as their spouse shares marriage "offenses," stop the companion to apologize and repent. How the Lord would like to hear something said softly like, "Wait—honey, do you mean that for years I have been insulting and sarcastic, hurting you like you have just described? It made me ill as I listened to you describe my behavior and its effect on you. I am really sorry. I know I can do better than that. If you still have any feelings for me, would you be willing to give me another chance? Please forgive me, if you can. I will do better, I promise."

Rarely do I see couples who are experiencing marital problems take individual responsibility for their sins and genuinely repent. And yet, if either one were administered a pencil-and-paper test on repentance about someone else who had done what they were doing, they would be able to see it much clearer. No wonder President Ezra Taft Benson said that pride is "a sin that can readily be seen in others but is rarely admitted in ourselves" (in Conference Report, April 1989, p. 5). We become blinded to our own faults, unable to see the beam in our own eye.

Imagine a neighbor saying to you, "My husband and I are not getting along very well. It looks like maybe we won't make it. I don't know what to do." What would your response be? Typically we would say something like, "You two really need a vacation. You need to get away together. You need some long talks. You must be under lots of stress." We might even take the side of the neighbor by saying, "Well, if he said those things to me, I'd feel the same way you do." We would probably *not* say, "You two have stopped praying together, haven't you?" (You can be certain they have stopped.) "Why don't you change your response to what he is doing?" "What can you do to correct the problem?" "Can you be less stubborn?" "Can you forgive your companion?" "Have you forgotten your covenants?" "Have you lost your charity for his weaknesses?" "What would the Lord tell you to do?"

Most of us don't think of these responses, but they might be more helpful and accurate than anything else we could say or do. We often fall into a pattern of encouraging people to separate or divorce because we accept their rationalizations and excuses for *not repenting.* There are justifiable reasons to break up a marriage, of course. But normally there are repeated transgressions by both parties. What is needed is for each to take responsibility for what he or she can and to then repent. Think in these terms: When was the last time you honestly, genuinely took responsibility for a temper tantrum, an inadequate performance, or any of a number of offenses and asked your spouse or child for forgiveness?

Repentance involves an honest, genuine request for forgiveness and a commitment to do better. It can't be faked; it must be bona fide. Certainly, risk is involved. Unfortunately, our tendency is to respond, "I am sorry, but . . ." and then to proceed to justify our emotional outburst. To repent, to take responsibility, to apologize for our offending behavior—this is difficult for most of us. That is why President Spencer W. Kimball said that selfishness was the basic cause of divorce, and President Ezra

Taft Benson labels pride as the great offender, for these traits do not lend themselves to apologizing, to sincerely changing and repenting. Pride does not yield to repentance, nor does it allow for taking responsibility for error. Pride only allows for wrongful justification of our actions and blaming those who we think are responsible for our inconvenience.

Though it is difficult for most of us to apologize to a spouse, it is doubly hard to ask forgiveness of our children. Why? I suppose because we are the parents! We are the authorities. We have more experience. Think back: has there ever been a time when you apologized to one of your children, perhaps for disciplining them wrongly, being too harsh, or publicly embarrassing them in front of their friends? When we come to acknowledge our mistake, we usually have rationalized that too and may say to our children, "Well, it just makes up for all the times you got away with it in the past!" We shrug it off. Consequently, our children do not learn to apologize or repent either, and our pride is passed on to the next generation.

Marital Intimacy as a Form of Validation

The Lord intended the sexual expression of love within marriage to be an important form of validation. Sharing our sexuality with our spouse is a powerful form of validation, for it means that we enjoy being close to each other and that we are pleased to be married to each other. Commitment is renewed. Love is expressed and strengthened. The world is right again! President Joseph F. Smith explained: "Sexual union is lawful in wedlock, and if participated in with right intent is honorable and sanctifying" (*Gospel Doctrine* [Salt Lake City: Deseret Book Co., 1939], p. 309). However, our relationship must be cleared of any debris if intimacy is to be a truly validating component of marriage. Sexual expression must occur in a context of genuine caring and sharing. Otherwise, there is a danger of exploitation or selfishness.

Let's say that Richard, in the earlier example, puts the TV on "mute" or turns it off and goes to help his wife resolve the problem with their son. He does so willingly and cheerfully. He listens carefully and replies in an understanding, caring, valuing way. The chances are increased that Jan will risk again when she needs help. She will see her husband as a partner who wants to be a good father, and her self-esteem will be enhanced because she is treated as if she is important and loved by her husband. Richard understands that his role as a husband includes being supportive of his wife. The fact that she called on him indicates her confidence and dependence on him to help her when she is in a jam. And Rich has shown that no ball game is more important to him than his role as a husband and father. It is these kinds of actions that create a loving, caring context in which marital intimacy can thrive.

Summary

People marry with the expectation that they will experience deep personal fulfillment through marital companionship and intimacy. How disappointed they become if little appreciation is expressed for their contribution to the marriage! By contrast, how thrilling family life can be when people validate each other daily! Many problems in family relations could be resolved if we were more positive and complimentary and quick to overlook the faults of family members.

Healthy couples risk openly with each other and respond to each other positively and therapeutically. Through repeated experiences, trust grows and self-esteem is increased. Sharing the experiences of life together is the true joy of marriage. Frequent and genuine doses of validation must be passed between all family members. When an individual learns that he can take risks with his or her spouse and child, a therapeutic environment is established in the home, and trust, charity, and love flow freely there.

In contrast, when tension and put-downs are the order of the day, feelings are hurt and risk-taking decreases rapidly. In time a couple might see their relationship as unrewarding, and eventually such feelings become the basis for divorce, affairs, or worse. Or some couples may simply avoid each other and the pain of being put down or criticized. They need to repent, meaning that *both* partners need to start treating each other as happily married people do and to stop doing those things that are uncharitable, un-Christlike, and destructive of relationships. As the Prophet Joseph Smith taught: "When persons manifest the least kindness and love to me, O what power it has over my mind, while the opposite course has a tendency to harrow up all the harsh feelings and depress the human mind" (*Teachings of the Prophet Joseph Smith,* sel. Joseph Fielding Smith [Salt Lake City: Deseret Book Co., 1938], p. 240). Eliza R. Snow recorded the following counsel that the Prophet gave the Relief Society:

> Beware of self-righteousness, and be limited in the estimate of your own virtues, and not think yourselves more righteous than others; you must enlarge your souls towards each other, if you would do like Jesus, and carry your fellow-creatures to Abraham's bosom. He said he had manifested long-suffering, forbearance and patience towards the Church, and also to his enemies; and we must bear with each other's failings, as an indulgent parent bears with the foibles of his children.
>
> . . . As you increase in innocence and virtue, as you increase in goodness, let your hearts expand, let them be enlarged towards others; you must be long-suffering, and bear with the faults and errors of mankind.
>
> . . . Let this Society teach women how to behave towards their husbands, to treat them with mildness and affection. When a man is borne down with trouble, when he is perplexed with care and difficulty, if he can meet a smile instead of an argument or a murmur—if he can meet with mildness, it will calm down his soul and soothe his feelings; when the mind is going to despair, it needs a solace of affection and kindness. (Ibid., p. 228.)

Of course, it works both ways, and at times we all need solace, affection, and kindness.

CHAPTER TEN

Eternal Families— A Unique Doctrine

Before serving as a mission president, I assumed that if I could just get my missionaries out among the people to explain the principles of marriage and family relations, scores of people would join the Church over this doctrine alone. I reasoned that there were many people like me—people who greatly loved their spouses and children—who wanted to know how they might secure their families to them forever. But I soon learned that there are many modern Sadducees to whom such a doctrine is beyond their present theological understanding and therefore acceptance. They look upon marriage and parenting as earthbound compared with their concept of heaven in the glorious presence of God.

As Latter-day Saints we are unique in our belief that family life does not end with death. Though the Savior has explained that "what therefore God [not man] hath joined together, let not man put asunder" (Matthew 19:6), there are many who do not understand his meaning. Too, there is a misunderstanding of a conversation found in chapter 22 of Matthew that takes place between Christ and the Sadducees concerning resurrection. Because many contemporary Christians draw false conclusions from this conversation, it is one of the primary reasons they do not accept the doctrine of eternal family relations.

President David O. McKay envisioned every member a missionary. Perhaps our strongest appeal to the world community might yet be the doctrine of eternal family life if we can have stable marriages and show the rest of the world the happiness that can come through marriage and children. We already are known for our interest in the family through the public-relations efforts of the Church. But our example as married companions and parents may be the key to a greater acceptance of the gospel by those not of our faith, particularly as the world struggles more and more with divorce and other problems within the home.

Since most contemporary Christian theology does not allow for the continuation of marriage and family beyond this life, we need to understand the context of this dialogue in Matthew if we are to assist our neighbors in understanding the restored truths about families. Immediate benefits would come to spouses and to their children if there were no misunderstanding on this doctrinal issue.

Jesus and the Sadducees

The Sadducees were a small sect of Jewish aristocracy who did not believe that man possessed an individual spirit or that human beings lived after death. "When you're dead, you're dead" was their conviction. However, to other Jewish groups of the day, notably the Pharisees, eternal marriage and family life were prominent articles of faith. (In some ways, modern Christians could learn from these early Jews.) Elder Bruce R. McConkie commented on the Jewish beliefs concerning marriage at the time of Christ:

> Indeed, almost the whole Jewish nation believed that marriage was eternal, and that parents would beget children in the resurrection. Those few who did not believe that marriage continued after death—and among such were the Sadducees, who could not so believe because they denied the resurrection itself—were nonetheless fully aware that such was the prevailing religious view of the people generally. . . .

The Sadducean effort here is based on the assumption that Jesus and the Jews generally believe in marriage in heaven. They are using this commonly accepted concept to ridicule and belittle the fact of the resurrection itself. (*Doctrinal New Testament Commentary*, 3 vols. [Salt Lake City: Bookcraft, 1965–73], 1:604–5.)

The issue of marriage was a current topic of discussion among Jewish sects. The Sadducees came to Jesus hoping that he would endorse their position. They had nothing to lose. If he sanctioned the Sadducean position, the larger and dominant Pharisees would turn against him. If he favored the position of the Pharisees, the Sadducees could dismiss him as a false messiah.

They approached the Savior on the issue of the resurrection this way:

Master, Moses said [in the law, Deuteronomy 25:5–10], If a man die, having no children, his brother shall marry his wife, and raise up seed unto his brother.

Now there were with us seven brethren: and the first, when he had married a wife, deceased, and, having no issue, left his wife unto his brother:

Likewise the second also, and the third, unto the seventh.

And last of all the woman died also.

Therefore in the resurrection whose wife shall she be of the seven? for they all had her [as a wife]. (Matthew 22:24–28.)

The Sadducees' intent was to ridicule the idea that such a thing as a resurrection could be a reality.

Before looking at the Savior's response to their question, I need to digress for a moment. Those who have served missions know that there are individuals who have no real interest in learning true doctrine, or finding out our beliefs on given issues. They would prefer to expound their own wisdom, combining scriptures with their own false philosophies and premises and often ridiculing our church and beliefs. Often these individuals are from fundamentalist evangelical churches, the saved-by-grace-alone camp who believe that a confession of Christ's name is sufficient to enter heaven. New missionaries to the field, perhaps unaware of the theological position of these individuals, think they can explain the correct doctrine to them and clarify our position.

The Savior, in contrast to inexperienced missionaries, understood Sadducean theology and knew the intent of his questioners. Therefore, he first rebuked them for their misconstruing the scriptures: "Ye do err [in your doctrine], not knowing the scriptures [which teach of a resurrection], nor the power of God [priesthood keys to resurrect men and women]" (Matthew 22:29). In effect he said, "Your theology is flawed. You have misinterpreted the scriptures, which testify of a Redeemer who will overcome the death brought upon mankind by our first parents. The resurrection is a free gift to all people through the Redeemer's infinite sacrifice." Because the Sadducees had used marriage as the vehicle to propose the question of resurrection, Christ explained, in essence, "As far as your question about marriage is concerned, because you do not accept the more basic concept of the resurrection, how could there be marriage beyond this life for anyone who does not believe in life after death?"

His answer was Sadducee-specific, of course, geared to their false theological assumptions and conclusions. He was not speaking to those who knew the correct doctrine of the resurrection and its implications for marriage and family life. The Savior had earlier taught the doctrine of eternal marriage (see Matthew 19:3–6) when the question of divorce was raised by the Pharisees. And unlike many young missionaries, Jesus chose to deal with the more fundamental question of the resurrection by pointing out the inconsistency of their question without an understanding of that doctrine. He knew the Sadducees were indifferent to his teachings and that their real intent was to trap him into a dangerous stance. He did not take the time to explain a doctrine incompatible with their theology, especially since the other sects of the day were not confused on the issue.

Jesus gave a stinging rebuke to them in reminding them of a more fundamental principle concerning his Father: God is not the God of the dead, but of the living. The scripture records, "But as touching the resurrection of the dead, have ye not read that which was spoken unto you by God, saying, I am the God of Abraham, and the God of Isaac, and the God of Jacob? God is not the God of the dead, but of the living. And when the multitude heard this, they were astonished at his doctrine." (Matthew 22:31–32.) Those hearing his reply were astounded at not only his rebuke of his questioners but his simple logic concerning God. Jesus told the Sadducees, in effect, "To show you how silly your position is of rejecting the resurrection, look at what you are saying: You read in the scriptures about the God of Abraham, Isaac, and Jacob; yet you say these great men are now dead, and that they will not live again. How could a living God be the God of the dead? I tell you that God is not the God of the dead. If they are no longer alive, then why speak of God as their God? If they are dead, they need no God. Your position is sadly absurd?" (The irony of this interchange between the Savior and the Sadducees is that they were speaking to the very Being who would bring about their resurrection as a free gift, regardless of their acceptance of him as the Messiah; for they would be resurrected, as will all men and women.)

Without understanding the teachings of the Sadducees and the context of this exchange with the Savior, Christians have assumed that Jesus was making a pronouncement that applied to everyone in the world—not just this sect. We have a more complete explanation of the principle of eternal marriage outlined in our latter-day scripture, one that refutes the position of the Sadducees:

> And everything that is in the world, whether it be ordained of men, by thrones, or principalities, or powers, or things of name, whatsoever they may be, that are not by me or by my word, saith the Lord, shall be thrown down, and shall not remain after men are dead, neither in nor after the resurrection, saith the Lord your God.
>
> For whatsoever things remain are by me; and whatsoever things are not by me shall be shaken and destroyed.
>
> Therefore, if a man marry him a wife in the world, and he marry her not by me nor by my word, and he covenant with her so long as he is in the world and she with him, their covenant and marriage are not of force when they are dead, and when they are out of the world; therefore, they are not bound by any law when they are out of the world.
>
> Therefore, when they are out of the world they neither marry nor are given in marriage; but are appointed angels in heaven, which angels are ministering servants, to minister for those who are worthy of a far more, and an exceeding, and an eternal weight of glory.
>
> For these angels did not abide my law. (D&C 132:13–17.)

Eternal marriage did not fit in the theological framework of the Sadducees. It would have required a major reordering of their thinking for them to accept what Jesus was saying, something the Savior knew they were unwilling to do.

The Lord explained to Joseph Smith the ennobling principle of eternal marriage in its correct context:

> If a man marry a wife by my word, which is my law, and by the new and everlasting covenant, and it is sealed unto them by the Holy Spirit of promise, by him who is anointed, unto whom I have appointed this power and the keys of this priesthood . . . whatsoever my servant hath put upon them, in time, and through all eternity . . . shall be of full force when they are out of the world; and they shall pass by the angels, and the gods, which are set there, to their exaltation and glory in all things, as hath been sealed upon their heads, which glory shall be a fulness and a continuation of the seeds forever and ever.
>
> Then shall they be gods, because they have no end; therefore shall they be from everlasting to everlasting, because they continue, then shall they be above all, because all things are subject unto them. Then shall they be gods. . . .
>
> Verily, verily, I say unto you, except ye abide my law ye cannot attain to this glory.
>
> For strait is the gate, and narrow the way that leadeth unto the exaltation and continuation of the lives, and few there be that find it, because ye receive me not in the world neither do ye know me. (D&C 132:19–22.)

Christ made it possible for families to be eternal through his atonement and resurrection. All individuals will be resurrected as male or female with a body of flesh and bone and spirit. Once resurrected, they will never die or have their bodies and spirits separated again.

This same issue is a major dilemma for many contemporary Christians, some of whom resemble the Sadducees. Others believe in Christ's resurrection but are blind to its application to marriage and family relations. Though they believe Christ is the Redeemer, they do not understand the significance of the Atonement's power to restore physical and spiritual bodies that possess male or female characteristics. Without an understanding of priesthood keys to seal couples together in a new and everlasting covenant of marriage, they face the dilemma of marriage being limited to this life only. Their theology does not allow for eternal family relations.

Most Christians view Christ's atonement as the instrument to bring about forgiveness of sin. That is, certainly, one of the most important dimensions of the Atonement. However, Latter-day Saint theology clarifies several other gifts we are given through the Atonement:

1. Restoration of the physical and spirit bodies together so that they will never be separated again (see Alma 11:45; D&C 138:17)
2. Retention of male or female attributes in the resurrected body
3. Retention of marriage and family relationships organized by priesthood power

If the Atonement does not have the power to accomplish these three things, together with enabling us to be forgiven of our sins if we repent, then it was very limited. Yet, Christ was the great example. His resurrection brought his body and spirit back together. He rose from the grave with masculine characteristics, with the obvious implication that females will be resurrected as females. Without the continuation of family life, earth life would be an exercise in futility. But this is precisely the belief of most modern Christians—that marriage and family are limited to mortality.

The restoration of truth concerning the atonement of Jesus Christ and its contribution to marriage and family relations is thrilling to every couple in love. It makes the calling of Joseph Smith as a prophet easy to accept, for without these principles being restored in our day we would be in the same position as other Christians. Marriage could be looked upon as a temporary phenomenon, and parenthood would not have the same significance. Individuals could justify never marrying, living together without marriage, not wanting to have children, or maintaining a whole host of false beliefs that exist in our culture. The Restoration clarifies the doctrine of eternal families and gives meaning and incentive to us to become the very best companions and partners we can be; parenthood becomes a wonderful privilege to work with Heavenly Father in bringing his children to this earth, and we are allowed to apprentice in anticipation of eternal increase (see D&C 131:1–4).

This doctrine of marriage and family has an antecedent. Even more basic than the doctrines of resurrection and marriage is the concept of God revealing his plan of salvation and his mind to men in our day as he did in times past. I speak of revelation, for it required a new dispensation of gospel principles and priesthood keys to restore the concept of eternal families. This is another principle not readily accepted by our contemporaries because their theology does not allow for post-Biblical revelation, which prevents them, much like the Sadduccees, from accepting the advanced doctrines pertaining to family relations. Without revelation on this and other matters, we would be stymied in moving the work of God forward.

President John Taylor gave a classic statement concerning the importance of revelation from God. He said:

> A good many people, and those professing Christians, will sneer a good deal at the idea of present revelation. Whoever heard of true religion without communication with God? To me the thing is the most absurd that the human mind could conceive of. I do not wonder, when the people generally reject the principle of present revelation, that skepticism and infidelity prevail to such an alarming extent. I do not wonder that so many men treat religion with contempt, and regard it as something not worth the attention of intelligent beings, for without revelation religion is a mockery and a farce. If I can not have a religion that will lead me to God, and place me *en rapport* with him, and unfold to my mind the principles of immortality and eternal life, I want nothing to do with it. (In *Journal of Discourses* 16:371.)

In the long run, Mormonism is for married lovers! It was designed to create forever families. Of all the truths vouchsafed to us in these latter days, these are among the most profound.

Parley P. Pratt said:

> It was at this time [during the winter of 1839–40] that I received from [Joseph Smith] the first idea of eternal family organization, and the eternal union of the sexes in those inexpressibly endearing relationships which none but the highly intellectual, the refined and pure in heart, know how to prize, and which are at the very foundation of everything worthy to be called happiness. . . .

It was from him that I learned that the wife of my bosom might be secured to me for time and all eternity; and that the refined sympathies and affections which endeared us to each other emanated from the fountain of divine eternal love. It was from him that I learned that we might cultivate these affections, and grow and increase in the same to all eternity. . . .

I had loved before, but I knew not why. But now I loved— with a pureness—an intensity of elevated, exalted feeling, which would lift my soul from the transitory things of this grovelling sphere and expand it as the ocean. (*Autobiography of Parley P. Pratt,* ed. Parley P. Pratt, Jr. [1874; reprint, Salt Lake City: Deseret Book Co., 1985], pp. 259–60.)

Eternal Life Is Not Automatic

Though we have lofty views and aspirations concerning the eternal nature of marriage and family relations, they can be valid only when two people are faithful to their covenants. No sealing is valid if one of the parties does not qualify for exaltation. Only those who become like Christ in their nature will be eligible for exaltation and continued family associations. So, our task as husbands and wives, fathers and mothers, is to develop righteous habits and characteristics that emulate the traits of the Savior so that we can be with our families throughout eternity. Simply having ordinances performed in sacred places, or merely tolerating each other amid sarcasm, cutting remarks, crudeness, and hurtful actions, does not lead to the highest of eternal possibilities.

Unfortunately, many behave as though all sins and transgressions will be forgiven at the Judgment as long as they were married in the temple. Individuals who retain such beliefs are in for a rude awakening! No one will be sealed to anyone else if either party does not qualify for eternal life.

It is Satan who would have men and women believe that marriage is limited to mortality, or that we are saved by ordinances alone. Remember that his great punishment is to be denied marriage and fatherhood. He will never have a sweetheart, nor be blessed with a son with whom he can wrestle, play ball, and ordain to the priesthood. He will never baptize his own boy, send him off on a mission for the Lord, or be present in the temple on the day his son marries a wonderful young bride of his own.

Satan will never have a little daughter he can bless to sleep through the night when she is suffering from sickness or fear. Nor can he ever read her a bedtime story or take her to the fair or circus. He will never be able to teach a young daughter simple gospel principles and perform priesthood ordinances in her behalf. He is damned as to marriage and family relations forever— and he is determined that you will not retain those powers or opportunities either. He will do all that he can to destroy your marriage, to prevent others from achieving what is denied him. He wants all of us to be as miserable as he is.

As family members we must retain the vision of the potential of our marriages and keep our covenants, or we may lose these wonderful privileges through carelessness. Every time a couple, married in the temple, divorces, Satan must laugh and rejoice that another couple has lost their way. Marriage and family relations are designed to exalt us, but some may instead choose to imitate the adversary. The choice is ours to make because the Atonement overcomes both physical and spiritual death and enables us to continue in eternity that which we have begun here.

This life is the great adventure for us to find an eternal partner and to live so that we might carry on this relationship forever. Married people who love and cherish each other have cause to rejoice: marriage can be forever.

CHAPTER ELEVEN

Married and Still Courting

When we see couples sitting next to each other in their car, strolling hand in hand down the sidewalk, or showing some other kind of affection in public, we usually conclude that they surely must be dating, not married. Why? Do married couples stop demonstrating affection for each other just because they are married? Have we lost the thrill of holding hands or sitting close together in the car? (It isn't the bucket seats, is it?) Does the novelty of marriage wear off so quickly that we soon become just like all the other "old fogies" around? Read the following and see how you compare to this couple:

The Seven Ages of the Married Cold

Year 1   "Honey, I'm really worried about you. You've got a bad sniffle and there's no telling about these things with all the strep going around. You jump in bed and I'll take care of everything."

Year 2   "Listen, darling, I don't like the sound of that cough. I've called Doc Miller and I'm off to get a prescription. I think you ought to relax a little. The house looks fine."

Year 3 "Maybe you better lie down, sweetheart. Nothing like a little rest when you feel lousy. After the dishes are finished I think you ought to hit the sack, don't you?"

Year 4 "Look, dear, be sensible. Take a couple of aspirin. There is no need to try to clean the whole house when you aren't feeling well. It'll still be here tomorrow."

Year 5 "Good grief, why don't you take a couple of Contac? You sound terrible?"

Year 6 "For Pete's sake, stop sneezing! You are going to give us all pneumonia!"

Year 7 "If you'd just gargle or something instead of sitting around barking like a seal, I'd appreciate it."

(Adapted from material presented in Dennis Rainey, *Lonely Husbands, Lonely Wives: Rekindling Intimacy in Every Marriage* [Dallas: Word Publishing, 1989], pp. 5–6.)

What will this couple be like after twenty years?

Here are some questions for you to consider: If marriage is all downhill after the ceremony, as many describe and predict, how would a husband and wife feel about each other after a few thousand years? (After all, that is where we are headed, isn't it?) Do we tend to see marriage as simply a game in which we use wonderful personality traits to trick another person into marrying us, only to revert to our core personality after we have won the prize? Do we find ourselves feeling "stuck" with each other, saddled with debt, responsibilities, and children so that there is no longer any joy left in our companionship? Are we so comfortable with each other that we no longer feel the flame of passion that ignited our matrimonial candle? Have we lost our enthusiasm for romance and all the crazy things we did to land each other in the first place? Has the "legality" of sexual intimacy caused us to not worry about any other expression of love and caring? Have sexual relations become the only way we express any affection for each other anymore?

What is the source of our happiness as married people? I hope we have not become so calloused as to draw such conclusions as this: "Well, he isn't going anywhere. We have been sealed in a temple marriage, and he would be excommunicated if he were to do something foolish, so why do I need to worry about my weight, health, manners, or about romance any-more?" Does the marriage ceremony presuppose that there is no further need to use the same skills after marriage that were so important before?

Shame on you if you are answering "yes" to any of these questions!

If we are not enriching our relationships when away from the marriage bed, not only are we missing a number of pro-found dimensions of love but we will also diminish that special time together. What happens away from the bedroom is just as important—no doubt more so—in enriching our marriages and meeting our personal goals for marriage. If husbands cease courting their wives simply because love and sex are "the same thing," how can their marriages grow? How can we develop bonds strong enough to withstand the inevitable challenges that are sure to test our commitment? What happens to our rela-tionship when sexual intimacy is restricted or impossible for health reasons, or when our aging bodies refuse to cooperate?

A lack of continued dating on the part of marital partners leads to a boring marriage. I hear many individuals, usually women, tell me how boring their marriage has become. "All my husband wants to do is to stay home, watch television, and then get me into bed," complained Susie. "I enjoy our intimate time together, but I like to think there are other things in life. I'm be-ginning to think that is all he married me for." If a couple had a bank account from which they only made withdrawals, the bal-ance would soon be exhausted. Daily deposits of love and kind-ness are essential if a marriage is to remain solvent, accumulate assets through wise management practices, and avoid bank-ruptcy.

President Harold B. Lee observed, "I say to you brethren the most dangerous thing that can happen between you and your wife is apathy . . . , for them to feel that we are not inter-ested in their affairs, that we are not expressing our love and sharing our affection in countless ways" (Regional Repre-sentatives' seminar, 12 December 1970). The same can be true for women who fail to validate their husbands.

Dating is an important part of marriage. Friday night dates have long been recommended to enhance marital relations. Finding a reliable baby-sitter to enable a couple to go out alone or with other couples at least once a week is an important part of strengthening marital relations. (If you are really poor, trade baby-sitting with another couple.) Couples must have time away from children and telephones to renew their companionship, to remind each other of their unique strengths as individuals and as a partnership, and to keep courtship alive and vibrant. Such excuses as "There isn't any time," "We can't afford it," "I've got too many things going," "We live in Dullsville," or "There is nothing to do" are weak.

Relationships are strengthened by spending positive time together, when each can share feelings about life and living. If married people are to be therapists to each other—one of the most important roles each plays—there must be time for that joint therapy. Building frequent memories together will be welcome deposits to the marital bank account. Strong relationships are not built on a single strength, such as sexual intimacy, but on a consistent exchange of a variety of investments in each other. If sex were the only attraction between two marrieds, it would be like playing a single note on the piano when the potential exists for an entire symphony. There is nothing as therapeutic as two committed, covenant people bouncing along arm in arm, continuing their courtship and watching their feelings of love bloom into a full, sweet-spirited, mature love that really is worthy of an eternal stamp.

"As the marriage goes, so goes the family" is more than a cliché. What could be more valuable to your children than for them to see the two of you happily married, deeply in love, and obviously caring about each other as you send verbal and non-verbal messages, praying out loud for each other and for them. Chances are improved that your own children will find happiness when you have set the example for how a loving, healthy couple behaves. When children see their parents embrace in full view, hear them express their mutual excitement to see each other after being apart, and are aware that their parents date regularly, attend the temple, treat each other with respect, and demonstrate the kindest of manners, how can they help but carry that same model into their own marriages? As President Harold B. Lee once said, "A woman happy with her husband is better for her children than a hundred books on child welfare" ("Be Loyal to the Royal within You," in *Speeches of the Year*

[Provo: Brigham Young University Press, 1974], p. 92). Where else can children observe a marriage up close, one that they would like to pattern their own companionship after? Certainly not from Hollywood or the soap opera myths. Example is the most important form of teaching the values and joys of matrimony. Some of your children's friends may have parents who divorce, and your children will always be grateful that you two "had it together."

When we do not set a positive example for our own children, a situation like the following, described by Elder Boyd K. Packer, can occur:

> Some time ago there came to my office a couple to meet an appointment that had been arranged by their stake president. They were in their early thirties; they had four children; they had been married in the temple, were nominally active in the Church.
>
> They had wrestled endlessly with some very difficult problems; had wept a great deal; had experienced a great deal of counseling, and had finally determined that they must get a divorce.
>
> There was no third party involved. There was no moral transgression. Life in their home was fraught with such problems that it became a literal and living hell for them. They could stand it no longer and had decided that as bad as divorce is, and as disappointing as failure would be, either of them was better than going on as they were.
>
> I invited the wife to tell me about the problem. As soon as she began to speak, the husband snapped at her, "Why don't you tell him the truth! You would even lie to a General Authority. Why don't you tell it the way it is!"
>
> I invited him to be quiet and listen while she had her say.
>
> He, in turn, was invited to speak and had not completed a sentence before she, in her icy bitterness, accused him of being the cause of all the trouble. Then I had to invite her to listen, if she would.
>
> They concluded and I was going to ask a question, but thought the evidence was clear and so made the statement, "Both of you came from broken homes, didn't you?" They both looked surprised, and then nodded their heads affirmatively. "Tell me about it," I invited.
>
> Each told me of the unhappiness and heartbreak of seeing their parents separate in divorce when they were little youngsters. The husband was about seven, and his wife, I believe, was about

nine when their families had broken up. Everything they had believed in and trusted, everything by way of security had fallen
apart before them. . . .

Almost by accident I asked a question of her. I said, "What is
it you want of him?"

And for the first time she became a woman. She started to
cry, her face softened, she seemed more like a little girl, and she
said, "All I want is for him to treat me like Brother 'Somebody'
treats his wife. That's all I want."

Now you know what she had seen. They would come to
Church . . . fighting, bickering, and miserable, complaining; then
Brother and Sister "Somebody" would come in with their little
family—a couple in love helping one another, and nudging one
another when their children did something. Well, you know what
she had seen. And somehow she knew that whatever that was, she
didn't have it in her marriage, and that is all she wanted.

I asked him what he wanted of her and he said, "All I want is
for her to be a good wife." Now, where would she learn to be a
good wife? In school? In a book? Imagine it? She had never lived
in a home where a wife showed the proper respect to her husband
or love for her husband, or where there was a feeling of warmth
and love.

And how would he ever know how to treat a wife like Brother
"Somebody" treated his? Imagine it? Dream it up? What book
could he read that in? What course in school would teach him
that? He had been deprived by the misfortunes of his parents and
now was paying the price and his little children—I remind you,
the third generation—were now to suffer the penalties.

It has been interesting to me that many couples who come for
help—some of them with grown children—haven't the vaguest
idea about some of the very basic considerations in the husband-
wife relationship.

Some women, long married, have no idea, it seems, about
how a man is put together, what his needs are, how he can be
lifted and inspired and encouraged.

And many men, though they have lived with a woman for
years, don't seem to have the faintest idea about what a woman
needs, how she can be inspired and made perfect. (*Eternal
Marriage*, Brigham Young University Speeches of the Year [Provo,
14 April 1970], pp. 3–5.)

How true this experience is for so many, especially for those
who have not grown up in a home where two parents exhibited

the kind of caring and love that would help their children learn how to succeed in their own marriages.

As for dating as married companions, here are some proven ways to enrich your marriage relationship, gleaned from my own marriage and those of others:

1. Build religious rituals into your companionship. Be sure to be consistent in your own individual prayers, your prayers as a companionship, and family prayer. Family home evenings are a must, for they provide time to build relationships—the key to family unity. Don't neglect them, or stop them just because the children are older and busier. You must find time together and as a family for scripture study and prayer. Even if it has to be during the dinner hour, make sure that you don't neglect these important things.

2. When you can afford it (or can find one in a garage sale or auction), buy a stereo system so that you can kick off your shoes and dance together at home or just enjoy your favorite tunes with each other. Listen to old songs that were played during your era.

3. Write separate accounts of how you two found each other, and make copies to distribute to all your children.

4. Foot-back-neck and head-leg-feet rubs are very therapeutic and soothing, especially when they are spontaneous and given as freewill offerings (no accounting on who is ahead or behind, and no hidden agenda).

5. Send to your spouse through the mail a real, bona fide love letter—mushy and gooey, filled with genuine reasons why you are in love with your spouse.

6. Extend frequent—and I mean daily—expressions of love. Remember our earlier discussion on validating. Give your spouse such messages as, "I am so glad I have you as my eternal partner," "You mean so much to me," "Thanks for being such a wonderful wife [or husband]," "I often think, 'What would I do if I didn't have you?'" There are many simple ways to verbally, and nonverbally, express your love to your spouse. Do it frequently and genuinely.

7. When in church, at dinner, or in any crowded situation, whisper a love message in your sweetheart's ear. A simple "I love you; I can't wait to get you out of here" will do.

8. Plant a tree together—a symbol of your love and friendship.

Give it lots of nourishment and care, and watch it grow as does your love for each other.

9. Call from work or home—not too frequently—to occasionally interrupt your partner and let him or her know what's really important in your life. (Earning a living is simply a means to an end. Our real priorities in life have to do with each other.)

10. While the kids are in school or at a neighbor's home, come home for lunch and a little time to yourselves. You can let your imagination fill in the rest.

11. What could be cozier than building a fire in the fireplace and reminiscing together about your lives, your love, your family, your goals. How fun it is to go through old photo albums to see how much you've accomplished and how much you've changed!

12. You probably have a VCR, certainly a TV. Check through the listings and come up with an "oldie but goodie" that was popular at the time you were courting and married. The commercials ought to give you sufficient time to make it "interesting" to be together.

13. Try having picnics in unusual places—in the woods, by a river or lake, or at the top of the office tower where you work, for example. Even a candlelight dinner at the kitchen dinner table or a lantern dinner in the backyard could make special memories for the two of you.

14. Search a map of your city or county and find a historic site that you have not been to together (or with the family). After a little reading or investigating, visit it together. Act as if you are still dating, arm in arm, skipping if your legs allow it and enjoying the wind in your hair.

15. Call a cab, or get a friend to drive you, and go to a movie. (You may have to save a little out of each paycheck, or use "windfall profits" to save up for special times together.)

16. Grab the bikes and go to a park, museum, or a play together. Play "follow the leader" and enjoy the ride. (Please wear a helmet.)

These ideas are simply suggestions. The principle is, if you are going to be in this relationship forever, why not do what happily married couples do? Enjoy each other—physically, emotionally, mentally, and spiritually—frequently, creatively, and *now!* Why not be different from all those old fogies whose vessels founder on the rocks of boredom or whose priorities are out of whack. You will have each other forever—why not act like it now so that you will get used to the idea. After all, you are in this adventure together. You deserve the best! As President Spencer W. Kimball used to say, "Do it," to which some might add, "Do it, now!"

Index